101 Executive Uses for a Square Camel

Rob Wherrett

101 Executive Uses for a Square Camel

and other lightbulb moments in problem solving

Rob Wherrett

Published by Reroq Publishing, Glasgow

First published worldwide in 2018

Copyright © Rob Wherrett 2018

The right of Rob Wherrett to be identified as author of this work has been asserted by him in accordance with the Copyright, Designs and Patents Act 1988.

ISBN 978-0-9561305-2-5

British Library Cataloguing in Publication Data

A CIP record for this book can be obtained from the British Library

All rights reserved. No part of this publication may be reproduced, stored on a retrieval system, or transmitted in any form or by any means, electronic, mechanical, photocopying, recording, or otherwise without either the prior written permission of the Publishers or a licence permitting restricted copying in the United Kingdom issued by the Copyright Licensing Agency Ltd, Barnard's Inn 86 Fetter Lane London EC4A 1EN. This book may not be lent, resold, hired out or otherwise disposed of by way of trade in any form of binding or cover other than that in which it is published, without the prior consent of the Publishers.

Designed and typeset by Reroq Publishing

FOREWORD

If you have picked up this book then it shows that you are curious about Creativity and what it can do for you. More importantly it shows that you are looking to add value to your organisation and life in new ways.

People like you often ask me how much doing this is really worth. I ask them to consider how much using Creativity might have improved things in the past. How long has that past been going on for you? How many years do you expect it to stretch into the future?

Professionals know that to maximise value they constantly have to be creative. Using creativity techniques and frameworks really does have a positive impact. It was December 2000 and in one short afternoon I saved my client, who were the Marketing Team at American Express (EMEA), over £250,000 by preventing resource being allocated to an unnecessary project. It was simply because they were trying to solve the wrong problem. That's typical of the outcomes I get all the time.

What if that happened just once a week for 10 years! You do the maths. Can you afford **not** to have a go? Pick up the baton and run with it - besides, in doing so, you will also have a lot of fun.

Rob Wherrett

Glasgow, 2018

CONTENTS

Why we need Square Camels   1
Do Executives need Square Camels?   2

What is Creativity?   8
Learning how to drive it   11

Communications   12

Why use a Method?   15

Types of Technique   21
Stop! Technique   *23*

How to Select a Technique   25

Understanding Creative Style   29
What kind of Creative Leader are you?   32

Cognitive Bias and Style   37
   Countering the bias   *40*
   Creating constraints   *43*
   More styles   *44*

Problem Analysis   49
Validation - part 1   *49*

Individual Analysis Techniques: 50
   Art of Listening   *50*
   Checklists (for Problem Definition)   *51*

Comparative Customer	51
Daydreaming	52
Five W's and H (The Reporter's Notebook)	52
Repeated WHY?	54
Flipping the Binoculars	55
Jump-starting the Experience	56
Magazine Rack	56
Mirroring	57
Morphological Analysis	57
Reframing	62
Sharing	62
Think Tech	63
Unfamiliarity	64
Group Analysis Techniques:	64
Boundary Examination	64
Embrace Constraints	65
Fishbone Diagram	67
Kepner-Tregoe	68
Validation - part 2	69

It's all about Metaphor   71

Secret (Confidential) Techniques:	72
Right Brain Drawing	74

Idea Generation   79

Finding a Harlequin Bat	79
Lateral Thinking	80
Individual Idea Generation Techniques:	81
Assumption Reversals	81
Attribute Listing	81
Checklists	83
Exaggerated Objectives	84
Free Association	85
Goal Reversal	86

Metaphors	87
Mirroring for idea generation	88
NLP Techniques	88
Private Brainstorming	89
Reversals	90
Self-hypnosis technique for problem solving	91
Group Idea Generation Techniques:	**95**
Brainstorming	95
Reverse Brainstorming	98
Brainwriting	98
Crawford Slip Writing	101
Human Sculpture	102
Laddering	107
Mind Maps	108
Rolestorming	109
Super Heroes	109
Wynectics	111
Big Group Stuff	**117**
Metaplanning	117
Open Space	118
Evaluation	**121**
Creative Evaluation	121
Monte Carlo Estimating	121
Sticking Dots	127
Weighting Systems	128

Farewell to the Harlequin Bat   130

Index   132

Why we need Square Camels

Have you ever seen a Square Camel? More to the point, have you ever used one? Well I have certainly done the latter and it was a great experience - shared, as it happens, by a bunch of people in Glasgow who were participating in a research project I was running on behalf of the university. So why do we need them?

Without such radical concepts, creativity cannot exist for long. Instead we fall back on doing what we have always done - which isn't going to get us far in life. So I want you to come on a journey that will explore how to develop your own Square Camel or maybe it will be a Harlequin Bat (an animal not an object), an Addictive Pig or a Glass Handkerchief. I've used all of these concepts at different times to crack some rather tricky problems. Their use comes under the heading of creativity and I'm going to show you how easy that is. Both how to do it and how to manage its use in your organisation, to solve the big or complex problems you face.

There has been a lot written on the subject of creativity in the last few years but very little of it from the perspective of a real practitioner. Someone, that is, who routinely uses creative approaches when dealing with problems and issues - even when the answer might at first seem blindingly obvious (it usually turns out differently).

Instead there are volumes written about how to connect to your inner creativity and the like. But these don't generally result in change taking place and more creative application in the workplace or elsewhere. The reason for this disconnect is simple - humans have great faith in their own abilities. Thus admitting that you don't immediately know the answer to a problem can be mildly embarrassing. Our ego takes a knock so we don't let it happen.

Instead we are going to take a different approach. Let's throw the problem at a mythical creature or pass it through some crazy machinery. Both of these methods will spit out something really useful.

And therein lies the key - being creative in business or life in general isn't about being the person with all the answers. Instead it's being the person who takes the time to follow creative processes that will deliver those answers - often in completely unexpected ways. It also takes courage.

Courage to admit that you don't know but are willing to find out. And that runs counter to the expectations that the more senior you are the more infallible you become. Indeed, as parents find out, they are often left standing by their kids. So we should try and come up with easy ways to overcome the obstacles to solving the complexities of life.

*Don't be fooled by the masses of books that simply offer lots of techniques - you **have** to understand what you are doing before you go 'shopping' for more. To use a cookery analogy, you need to understand the basics before you start trying exotic recipes galore. Just choosing a book full of techniques can get you into a lot of trouble - the mindset has to change as well as what you actually do. Besides, as you will see, this is about embedding creativity into everyday and any good cook doesn't need to keep reaching for a recipe book.*

Do Executives need Square Camels?

Welcome to reality. The more senior you are - the less you are likely to have a handle on everything under your remit. It simply isn't possible to be that much of an expert. But the senior executive who understands how to use creative approaches and what those entail is far more likely to get to better answers across a wide range of subjects. Moreover, as you will see, they will have confidence that the answers are actually **right** because they will have been strength-tested against the underlying problems and the resources available.

There is another side to all of this - it is the hierarchy of Knowledge, Creativity and Innovation. As you go up the scale each becomes more complex. **Knowing** consists of storing in your head what is available elsewhere. **Creativity** relies on you imagining what isn't available elsewhere. **Innovation** requires creativity to actually work in context.

Just think for a moment what this means for you or your organisation. We readily accept knowledge - it's often doing what we've always done or know. But to what extent do you imagine possibilities? And, having imagined, do you synthesise according to context in order to innovate? That is why it is important to embed creativity in everyday processes. To challenge and imagine. To accept that nobody is the owner of absolute truth - no matter how powerful the CEO might appear to be.

In my career I spent many years building quality processes in organisations to ensure that what was being delivered addressed the complex issues at stake. Whether that was designing financial products; running change programmes; or developing software solutions to operational processing. The first question I always asked was *"what is the problem we are trying to solve?"* Then I asked it repeatedly until everybody agreed and the nuances had been flushed out. Only then did we set about building the solutions - but in their way they were often market leaders.

My experiences on being called in to other organisations are starkly different. In 100% of cases the problems they had been trying to solve were not the precise problems that were at the root of the issues. Yes, you read that correctly, **in 100% of cases**. It sometimes took a little tweaking but more often a radical rethink to get things on the right track.

Why was that? Well the answer usually lay in an instruction that was handed down from on high to do X. Not an instruction to find out the root cause of the underlying problem or the adverse effects on the business. Instead there was a defined solution that just had to be implemented as fast as possible. That, as explained above, is merely knowledge of the existing - and most likely it is imperfect knowledge at that. Small wonder that a vast majority of projects fail to deliver the projected benefits.

Don't take my word for it. In 2004 the Royal Academy of Engineering and the British Computer Society published a report titled *The Challenges of Complex IT Projects*. At that time only 25% of such projects were delivering the required outcomes. Most overran in terms of time or cost (or both) and didn't actually deliver what was intended even when they had finished. There hasn't been a significant improvement in the intervening years since publication. Look at the following quote from someone else and see if you agree.

> *"Common reasons quoted for project failure include: poorly specified technical requirements, poorly understood scope of work, over-complex designs, lack of detail within the design information, inadequate planning, inadequate budgetary controls, lack of communication, poor co-ordination and of course (the current favourite) weak leadership.*
>
> *While these conclusions may be an accurate, if generalised, representation of events, this type of causal analysis is akin to reporting that the weather is bad due to rain, hail, sleet or snow - all very obvious but in no way indicative of the true failure mechanisms that produced these effects."*
>
> Dr Steve Paton, University of Strathclyde
> Graduate School of Business

There is a saying in the military that *Planning and Preparation Prevents Poor Performance* (although being the military they often added a few extra P's for good measure). And with good reason. Think of the planning that went into *Operation Overlord* (the Normandy invasion on D-Day) or more recently the relief of Kuwait in *Desert Storm*. Even in both these cases there were gaps relating to the follow-up.

Yet somehow the civilian sphere of business pays little regard to such diligence unless they are forced to do so by legislation. Banks could (and arguably should) have dealt with the sub-prime mortgage business before it all collapsed in 2008. Yet only now are they doing things differently because governments have legislated and regulators are carrying out stress tests.

The same point could be made about building regulations and practice leading up to the catastrophic fire at the Grenfell Tower in North Kensington, London in June 2017. The list of failures to do the right thing is a very long one.

The consequences of not asking the right questions and being prepared to challenge can be huge. And often the people who end up paying have no say in the process. So being more creative in solving problems is of huge value to everyone. I'd go as far as to say it's what is missing nearly all of the time.

Way back in 1990 I was attending a training course just outside Bristol and was introduced to a selection of creativity techniques by the visiting speaker. I was hooked on just how rich the ideas were that they delivered. From that point onwards I started to use them in all sorts of situations. I also spent a good deal of time researching how they worked and finding ways to introduce them in a variety of organisations.

At the time I was a senior marketer for a Financial Services company and one day I passed Barry, one of our actuaries, on my way to the canteen for lunch. He asked, casually, if we had any radical new products in the pipeline as he wanted to test some new actuarial software to see if it would cope with them. I'd like to point out that at this time the internet had hardly been developed - we were still in the age of Microsoft Windows 3.1.1 and no graphical interfaces.

An hour later Barry had a written proposal on his desk which effectively predicted internet banking and customers managing their own investment accounts online. And all because I used the creative method and a random stimulus (a garden seat) suggested by Kevin, my junior assistant, who was with me in the lunch queue.

It's not just reading about bright ideas from James Dyson[1] or László Bíró[2]. This stuff works. It works all the time. And I've learned to trust it implicitly. Therein lies the difference between this book and all the others. You will have to get to grips with changing how you operate but not trying to be someone else.

I've read plenty of people who point out how some inventor or radical thinker has seized on a topic and turned it into a revolutionary product. What they don't do is point out **how** the original thinkers **failed to build creatively**. Yet in most cases they could. Of course technologies aren't always immediately available - as in my product design above. But all the parameters that the idea entailed could be worked on and in many cases the technologies can be adapted. My version initially suggested linking to bank cash machines as the user interface since these were the only widely-available connected devices.

One final example - and this time it's from UK Central Government. I was working with the UK Immigration Service redesigning their processing to deliver radical cost savings, particularly in the areas of Visa Applications and Asylum Casework. The proposed work stream was going to take two years or more and had a price tag of over £2 million just to build the required software. What was needed was a decision engine that could ask lots of questions and, depending on the answers, automate the response. You come into contact with this stuff on a regular basis without realising it. It's how banks decide on lending for one thing and the process is called underwriting.

I happened to know that an underwriting engine was available off the shelf for around £600k and could be implemented in around 3 weeks. That would have involved configuring the questions and algorithms to produce the

---

[1] James Dyson - UK inventor of the bagless vacuum cleaner amongst other things

[2] László Bíró - who invented the ballpoint pen.

correct decisions. So I suggested to the directors that they should consider this as a much faster and cheaper solution. The reply was telling. *"You don't understand. We are dealing with Immigration questions not insurance. It won't work."* And that was that - except that their preferred solution never got delivered even three years later with huge cost overruns along the way.

This inability to challenge preferred solutions to the wrong problem is at the heart of creative problem solving. Get it right and you save a bucket of money or other resources. More to the point the results tend to work better and sooner so it takes a lot of stress out of the organisation.

I'm a great fan of stress-free work. You should be as well - it's really a no-brainer. And using creativity properly, which means getting your people to use it as well, is a really worthwhile thing to do. Forget all the talk about work-life balance. This tends to deliver it without all the angst. People make better decisions sooner. This leads to better business conditions and in turn that feeds into the bottom line. Ultimately you can afford to work fewer hours and allow more focus on being human.

I eventually went on to work as a visiting Fellow with the Open University Business School for more than 16 years. I was teaching practical aspects of Creativity Techniques and how to select and apply them, to students from all over the world who were on the MBA Programme. We had a lot of fun along the way. However I also got feedback from time to time about the huge difference this was making in organisations across the planet.

So this is not a theoretical approach you are going to read. It's hands-on stuff that anybody can get to grips with and use. And even if you are not going to be facilitating any workshops just knowing about how this works means you can guide and encourage those working for you. Just remember - it's cool to say you don't know. It's even cooler to ask the difficult question WHY? Simply remember to step back and delve deep before launching into a solution.

What is Creativity?

Many people, when they think of creativity, automatically assume it has something to do with the media or the arts. What do **you** think? Where is there creativity in the world?

In my experience it comes in all shapes and sizes: from quick fixes to problems of customer service; to product design; or organisational change programmes. Simply put, creativity is everywhere and if you or your organisation isn't set up to handle it then you can bet your competitors are.

Tudor Rickards[3] defines creativity as *"the personal discovery process, partially unconscious, which leads to new and relevant insights"*. He also advocates a view of creativity as a universal human process resulting in the escape from assumptions and the discovery of new and meaningful perspectives, or as an *"escape from mental stuckness"*. In broad terms he believes creativity is to do with personal, internal restructuring.

I've heard of people who say their organisation hasn't got the time to be creative - they are too busy in the here and now. My immediate response is that is *"utter rubbish"*. Which board of directors wants to see a 75% waste of resources? Sadly that's what this short-termist approach is leading to.[4] If you are directing your people to fix things without going through the due diligence of finding out what the problems really are, then it's like buying a tumble dryer to dry your hair.

It really is that simple. There can be absolutely no excuses on this dimension. So make up your mind as a senior person in your organisation that you won't put up with this any longer. Then tell everybody why.

---

[3] Rickards, Creativity at Work (1988) He is Professor of Creativity and Organisational Change at Manchester Business School

[4] Think back to the research from the RAE on page 4. If less than 25% of change projects fully achieve the desired outcomes - failing to get this right may mean up to 75% of resources are misdirected.

In other areas, there are those who don't consider themselves creative. Really? You mean you never fixed a problem in your life? A lot of people point at others as being creative whereas they think they are not. It's a feeble excuse that's like saying only Formula 1 drivers can drive a car. It's utter nonsense. Of course, in driving, we don't all speed at 180mph around a circuit. Similarly in creativity we have different speeds and styles of getting there.

And it's no use insisting that you are a lawyer/accountant or whatever and that there is no room for creativity in your work. I remember dealing with the Head of Finance at a FTSE-100 retailer that was undertaking a change programme in their merchandising area. The aim was to stop buying excess stock, thereby saving money and bank interest. The Head of Finance just didn't understand that to get people to change they have to want to do so. His version was *"just tell them to do as they are told"*. Needless to say there were no creative approaches there and the whole attempt to do things differently fell flat on its face. If he had exhibited the slightest interest in trying things differently he would have saved his company £millions - and they might still be in the FTSE-100.

And here's a funny thing. Whilst many people will insist that we are all wired for creativity you don't need to understand how or why that works. Do you really understand how your laptop or tablet operates beneath the surface? Who cares? What you really need to know is how to use the tools it offers.

The same applies to getting creative. Use some tools and trust them to do what it says on the tin. That way you are tapping into your own internal capacity to be creative without having to understand the mechanisms at play. As time goes by you will start to become more intuitive in the way you approach creative challenges. That is no different to the first stumbles of texting and look at how fast you can do it now.

And talking of using a tablet or phone brings me to the idea of swiping. It's called creative swiping when you take an idea or process from somewhere else and just modify it for your own use. People do it all the time and the more creative people do it much more than average. It's quite helpful because you can look at what is going on in the existing world and start to model how it might be rather than starting completely from scratch.

Be honest - we all do a bit of cut and paste when we are writing a report. Reinventing the wheel all the time is a waste of effort. The critical thing is to be aware of when to go right back to basics. A gross error check on what you propose never goes astray. Is this an identical problem or is there something fundamentally different? The creative person will naturally go and check. If that's not you - then make sure someone does it. And that's a key to creativity - making sure these kinds of things are not simply ignored. That's the quick route to nowhere.

My own view, for what it's worth, is that you need to understand how the Creative Problem Solving (CPS) cycle works and develop a small number of tools that you or your team can use that are quick, portable and repeatable. Only when you can see that these are not getting anywhere should you have to reach for a library of more complex techniques. Hence the techniques shown in this volume are a mere subset of what's out there. But they offer enough to get people out of most corners and on the way to somewhere considerably better.

For the executive who is keen to make sure the organisation is using creativity there's enough here to get sufficient flavour. You can encourage people to dig deeper and research other ideas and tools once they've got the basics right. Otherwise it begins to feel like being creative requires lots of specialist techniques and knowledge and that defeats our objective of getting it ingrained.

I rather like the following quote from Karen Dillon, the former editor of Harvard Business Review:

> *"When a customer is settling for deeply imperfect or going to great lengths to try to get something done, you've identified a rich vein for innovation."*

That's just crying out for some creativity but if you know what the customer is actually doing then the next step isn't usually rocket science. What we are going to do is explain how you can identify problems and their causes. And then come up with practical ways of fixing them.

That is creativity at work in the workplace or, indeed, in your private existence. After all, most of this concerns human behaviour and - unless I'm very much mistaken - we don't shed our human existence when we leave the office (or the house). In fact one of the things about creativity is making connections from wherever they might come. Knowing that the boundaries don't stop at the office door or the loading bay is a good way of thinking.

Another great concept that helps along the way is to be playful. Don't get me wrong - this is actually a serious business but having a light heart and a few laughs or smiles actually helps us to relax. When we **are** relaxed our brains tend to be more open to new ideas and concepts. So there's a lot to be said for encouraging playfulness in your team when they are setting out to tackle something.

In fact those senior managers who are deadly serious all the time seldom achieve greatness. A sobering demeanour suppresses creativity in those around them - which hardly bodes well in the long term. It is a well-known element in the executive's portfolio of skills to be able to deal with the issues with which they are faced by using creativity to the benefit of the organisation. And it is precisely this aspect of the executive skill-set that is hardly ever taught on the job.

Learning how to drive it

In all of this there is one thing I want you to remember. Being creative is open to everyone. Learning to drive the Creative Machinery is no more difficult than learning to drive a car. So you might regard the rest of this book as a series of driving lessons. And, like driving a car, a lot of it becomes routine quite quickly.

Communications

This is a critically important area in Creative Problem Solving and yet is frequently overlooked. One of the things that can go wrong is that we predicate communications on the assumption that people understand what we are trying to communicate. How can they? Their perception of the reality is so different from our own as much as we all differ in Creative Style, as discussed in the chapter beginning on page 29.

For instance they may not have experienced working with a Square Camel or any of the other rich and rewarding things we know about. So we may have to help them into our world of perception - without the aid of mind-altering drugs or a crate of beer!

I'd also like to mention one other serious consideration about communication and how that impacts change. In Kirton's work on the Adaption-Innovation inventory (see page 45) he found that the **relative** position of individuals on the scale gives rise to problems in communication. (The scale runs from 32 - 160 in an approximately normal distribution with a mode around 95, so that leaves plenty of room for these sorts of differences to appear.)

Essentially once two people are more than 5 points apart it becomes noticeable, even more so towards the edges of the scale. At 20 points the communication becomes impossible. The reason? Their differing ways of perceiving the world interferes. You don't need to administer the inventory to find out who is where - simply look out for the tell-tale indications of how people view each other. Then do something to bridge the gap.

The relative Adaptor will tend to view the Innovator as abrasive or arrogant and has difficulty following their train of thought. (This applies even if both parties are towards the Adaptive end of the spectrum.)

Conversely the relative Innovator will wonder why what they are saying isn't obvious to the Adaptor. They then can get impatient at the apparent stupidity (which isn't actually real - merely the different cognition at work). So you have to manage communications in change very carefully and spend time making sure that everyone understands where you are going and why.

Yet how often do you recall anybody paying such attention to how to communicate and mitigate the problems? The more common approach is to tell people what they are going to do - the solution handed down from on high. They are expected to understand how that was arrived at - and frequently are not given any insight whatsoever.

It's also a common failing between areas such as Marketing or R&D who come up with novel solutions. These people tend to be towards the Innovative end of the spectrum for their organisation and yet the implementers of any solutions are likely to be in Operations. On the whole expect them to be slightly towards the Adaptive end of the continuum. This results in a classic cognitive divide and therefore what gets executed may not be what was intended unless someone put in the effort to bridge the gap.

Belief systems can also have an impact - particularly with large groups. If you are trying to engineer change how do you get someone to suspend his or her beliefs just to suit you? Should you even try? We must accept that people will only do what they really want to do and also that their belief systems will have a habit of getting in the way.

Here I am not concerned about the rights or wrongs of any particular system of beliefs. My own beliefs are just that. What is critically important is that we should not start to implant our own beliefs on others. On the other hand, by allowing others to see that you accept their own belief systems without prejudice, they begin to allow that your own beliefs may not be as threatening as they at first perceived. They do not have to accept a change of belief, merely a suspension of their own prejudice.

However, as we have seen earlier, we cannot expect to tell people to suspend their prejudices. We have to create the open space that will allow them to do so of their own accord. We know that space is a huge void and once in it all sorts of things are possible that are not 'down on earth'. We might use the metaphor that on earth gravity keeps everything anchored (at least most of the time) whereas, in space, zero gravity means that things can float alongside each other in ways that would otherwise be impossible.

You need to remember that people only take in about 11% of what they are told. Everything else comes from different modes of communication. Those might be kinæsthetic, visual, smell or taste. So handing out written instructions isn't the answer. It will be the right thing for some people - we'll deal with this in more detail when we look at Styles - but definitely not for others! And don't forget that some people are not good at delivering certain types of communication either. That's why you need a blend.

One of the things the clever manager will do is build a model of what needs communicating and then work out a matrix of delivery methods. That can be anything from Story Boards to Posters, Presentations or Q&A sessions. Food can even be involved - getting people together over a quick buffet or some snacks can change the mood and make them more receptive. The whole point is you are doing all this to bring people on board and get them working together on the right solution to the right problem.

Why use a Method?

Using a method makes things routine. The sort of things that remove the excuse of *"I'm not creative"* or *"we haven't time for this stuff."* Organisations rightly expect staff to follow certain routine procedures - so why not build CPS into them? Frankly it's bonkers not to. One bad decision that diverts resources can sink a business.

There's another reason why I take this so seriously. It works. And here's **why** it works. Just think for a moment about driving a car. Most people get a licence and learn to drive. Whilst they do so they are getting adept at internalising processes that will make it easy. Foot on clutch, change gear. Mirror, signal, manœuvre in traffic. And so on. And the more driving you actually do the more you forget about having to do these things. They become routine and you can start to focus more on the traffic around you and anticipate what is going to happen next.

So if just about anybody can learn to drive (or undertake some other complex activity on a regular basis) then anyone can embed creativity processes into their everyday work. It is actually easier than learning to drive. For one thing there isn't a ton of moving metal that might cause some damage to contend with whilst you do it.

Other writers will point you in the direction of psychological states, how to achieve or maintain them. These undoubtedly would improve the likelihood of creativity occurring. But let me ask you a very simple question. When do you ever follow an instruction manual? Honestly?

Most people actually get a broad grasp of how something is going to work and get on with using it. If it is a productive tool, then it will continue to be used and become an old friend. Reliable, understood and non-threatening.

Contrast that with trying to change your whole behaviour - whether that's doing meditation regularly or getting to the bottom of some psychometrics and reworking yourself as a consequence. People simply don't engage to that extent. Of course there are exceptions but on the whole it's too much of a hassle. So the method of embedding creativity has to be easy, require little personal effort and be productive.

Creativity experts the world over broadly agree that there is a cycle to Creative Problem Solving (CPS). And let's not forget that the whole point of being creative is to solve some sort of problem. This CPS Cycle covers four broad phases:

1. Problem analysis
2. Idea Generation
3. Validation
4. Execution

Importantly each of the phases starts by using divergent techniques before narrowing things down. In the Problem Analysis this consists of researching the facts and exploring all possible causes and relationships before distilling the problem to one or more statements.

When it comes to Idea Generation for solutions it helps to produce a wide variety of approaches. For one thing this may give additional insight. Just doing what you have always done rather than considering alternatives isn't necessarily going to deliver great outcomes.

Validation needs to be rigorous. As pointed out in the Case Study (3) below - potentially failure to do it could be fatal.

Finally, moving into the Execution phase is typical of starting any business project. That needs a solid plan, resource management and risk mitigations. In Monte Carlo Estimating on page 121 we look at some ways of tying this all together. Even this phase will start by exploring all the possible components before structuring them into a defined plan with resources and timetable.

The whole looks like a series of diamonds:

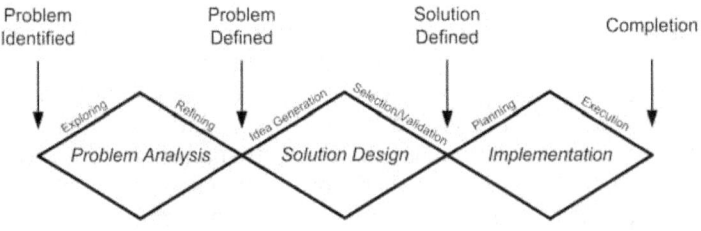

Case Study (3) :

This isn't strictly about CPS but it makes the point about trusting the process brilliantly. Working with a very large catalogue retailer there was a turnaround programme getting underway. Profits had slumped to almost zero on a turnover of £1.3bn so something had to be done. Various groups of managers were rightly looking for projects to undertake that would cut costs or otherwise improve the bottom line.

One morning about 20 managers were gathered in a meeting room to discuss a project in the supply chain that would deliver some improvements. On examination it appeared that the cost of the project would be about £500k and deliver £20 million in cost savings - after about three years.

When asked what their next step was going to be they just said *"We'll get started straight away."* However the routine process was to put the proposal to the Board for approval. When asked why they were not proposing to do this they said *"It's a no-brainer, the Board are guaranteed to like it so we won't bother asking them."*

When told that they had to follow the process they were stunned - until it was pointed out that £20 millions of benefit in 3 years time could cost them the business whereas the Board might have a better use for £500k in the short term.

> Result - one bad decision stopped dead in its tracks and valuable resource was not wasted.
>
> Having a good problem definition process identified the issue and investigation had delivered a comprehensive idea of solution. Following CPS logic the solution should have been validated against resource implications. Had that validation (Board sanction) been allowed to slip then chaos might have ensued. 20+ managers also got the message very quickly that rigour in applying this stuff might save their skins - so they didn't repeat the (near) mistake. So you see being good at CPS isn't a waste of time - far from it. You simply cannot afford to ignore it and assume that you don't have the time, energy or expertise.

Another key aspect of using CPS method is that it helps to know where you are in the process. From time to time you may have to loop back if things aren't going to plan. It is also important not to combine phases. For instance you cannot simultaneously be investigating cause and ideating a solution. That's not to say that possible solutions cannot be noted along the way but only with the proviso that until the problem is properly understood they are merely suggestions that **might** have relevance.

This combining is actually quite a common failing in organisations and should be among the first things you root out to get people on the right track. The reason it occurs is that people always think that getting to solutions quickly is clever. What you begin to understand is that getting to the **right solution** is clever and frequently takes a little longer to identify. That said, when it comes to the overall timeframe, getting to the right solution is likely to take less time than having to rework the wrong one.

Problem Analysis

We start with some notion that things need attention. Something isn't working as expected or there is a stimulus for change. But you shouldn't just accept that as being the right answer to the question *"what is wrong?"* Instead there is a period of investigation where all aspects of the issue are probed. Go wide and deep until there is a very full set of data. Only then does it make sense to start narrowing this down.

Complex problems are usually not singular in their causes. Instead we are dealing with interrelated issues, each with several possible causes. Therefore digging deeper is going to spread those out and we can examine each individually and look at the interactions before we decide where to start.

Finally we come to the point where we may have broken the problem down into its components and have one or several basic starting points. That is important to know because fixing one alone isn't going to solve anything - on the contrary it might makes things much worse. The wise problem-solver knows to treat each separately until all the potential solutions are on the table, then it will be the validation stage that works out which to tackle, how and in what order.

So in order to get to this stage, Problem Analysis goes through two phases. First a divergent phase to seek all the implications and possible causes and interactions. This is followed by a refinement to get to a precise Problem Definition.

Let's look at an example.

> A major retailer knew that they were having problems with their Merchandisers overbuying stock. They thought the problem was merely the process that the people were expected to follow. On investigation it appeared that this process was neither well-documented nor understood. At this point the management reaction was simply to tell the people to follow it.
>
> However deeper analysis revealed that there were conflicting messages hitting the Merchandisers from the Sales Team and Finance. More digging got to the bottom of the fact that the Sales Director

wouldn't engage with operations to communicate what he was trying to achieve. Without his input there was no impetus for his area to insist on the merchandising process being followed. And since they were not calling for information early in the buying cycles, nobody felt inclined to provide it. Instead silos were being developed where one part of the buying operation hadn't a clue how they were impacting the rest.

Validation started to weed out the noise and the underlying problem became clear. It was lack of communication from the Sales Area that was failing to drive the proper processes of buying. Yet an external consultancy had already redesigned the process without taking this into consideration and the Finance Team were tearing their hair out, insisting that you just have to tell people what to do and it will all be OK. That was the problem they should have been focused on solving - only they didn't and therefore wasted a pile of money on process redesign that simply wouldn't take hold.

Finally there is a rather delightful way of thinking about getting the Problem Definition right. It says that If you don't know where you're going, any road will take you there. But, as we know, any road might also end up in a cul-de-sac. Being clear about your true goal is the key to leading change.

Types of Technique

Let's be clear about these - I didn't invent any of the techniques other than a version of *Mirroring* (page 57) and the synthesised variant *Wynectics* (page 110). But you can't pretend that people only use the techniques with formal approvals from their original authors. Life isn't like that. Those listed here are brief summaries and I've tried to show what ingredients you need and the method of using them. It's a bit like a recipe book in that regard - the version of sponge cake in any cook book isn't necessarily attributable to one source. If you don't like 'my' version - go to another recipe and see if that works better for you. However those here have been personally tried and tested - mostly with people who are not themselves experts. So in that regard it's a pretty sound starting line-up.

There are lots of versions out there - whether you search for them on Google, YouTube or in Wikipedia - you will find many slight variants or descriptions of 'how to'. What you **should** try and do is devise a palette that works for you and your people.

I've broken them down into a few categories (although some work across categories so I've put those where they are most commonly found). Once you get the hang of it you can start to improvise and synthesise according to the particular circumstances you are dealing with.

Problem Analysis
These techniques are most frequently used to analyse problems and get to the underlying issues.

Idea Generation
Generating ideas from cold or by conversion from an existing idea, these techniques all have one thing in common - to develop new and varied ideas about possible solutions to a defined problem.

Validation

Making sure that the solutions proposed are checked against resource constraints, feasibility and preference(s) requires techniques to validate them. They include voting (for preferences) or various forms of measurement such as weighting.

Individual Techniques

These are predominantly used by a single person either in problem analysis or idea generation. Sometimes they can be used for either; but in this book they are listed where they are most frequently used in practice. Mind-mapping is a case in point - also it can be an individual or a group activity.

As a result these Individual Techniques can often be carried out almost anywhere.

Group Techniques

On the whole these require a modest number of people to be effective. The actual numbers can vary quite widely but 6-12 people is a good rule of thumb to begin with unless it is noted that the group size should be much larger (as in Meta Planning).

Some group techniques also require space or materials that may constrain their use.

Nominal Group Techniques

Just what is a nominal group? Well to put it simply everyone does their own thing (whether that's entering data; voting or something else) but the results are collated to give a group answer. They are often used when it is difficult to get everyone in the same place and may use digital connectivity or other mechanisms to capture the inputs. Questionnaires using an online tool such as SurveyMonkey would be a good example once the answers are collated.

One of the key things to remember about Creativity Techniques is that there are very few hard and fast rules. Yes be rigorous in your problem analysis and validations but the techniques themselves can morph and combine.

Wynectics (see p.110) is a case in point. It is a blend of several other techniques and is synthesised from the classical version of *Synectics*. But the key is that **it works!**

Stop! Technique

I've put this here for a simple reason. It is a technique on its own that can get you out of an awful lot of mess. It works in groups but can also be used by an individual (see alternative uses below).

It's fairly common for people in a meeting to pick things up at different pace. Sometimes they just need a pause to allow their brains to catch up or maybe they need a little clarity on a point that is complicated. This will help.

Requirements:
Nothing - just make sure everybody knows how this works and, if it is not commonly used, simply explain how it works at the beginning of the session.

Method:
Anyone can call **"Stop!"**

When they do, everyone stops talking/writing and takes **three deep breaths** focusing on the air going in and out. This is the STOP working.

Next the facilitator or others turn to the caller and ask *"Why?"* They may say they want clarification; or that they just need to mull the point over for a minute. Whatever they ask - the group **must** acknowledge and give them the space. Perhaps the facilitator will use some checking questions to ascertain whether the caller has the correct understanding of the point. Only when the caller has agreed can things move on. This may be by deferring a particular issue to a separate time but often the mere insertion of a pause allows them to catch up.

What you must NOT do, after the initial call and the three breaths, is simply to go back to the discussion/activity. That completely defeats the objective.

This is such a simple exercise that can defuse potential chaos in all sorts of meetings. Getting it practised by your teams is a great idea. No stigma is attached to the caller - everyone is buying in to the need to ensure that nobody gets left behind. I've personally used it in the boardroom as well as the workshop and it always does what is needed.

Alternative uses:

This can break annoying trains of thought - maybe you just cannot get a tune out of your head and that is stopping you concentrating on the job in hand. Stop! works by breaking the cycle in the brain - the deep breathing calms things down. In addition you might use it to avoid turning over something in your mind. For instance something has happened that is upsetting or annoying and you need to put it to one side.

All this is being creative. You are acting to achieve a different outcome than would otherwise follow from the general activities that are occurring.

How to Select a Technique

What is appropriate and where/when to use any particular technique can be confusing. So let's consider what the parameters ought to be and how you can then use those to define what's best.

First of all, is the problem fairly straightforward? If the answer is YES then it is likely that you don't need to do anything special to get to the root and deal with it. For instance there are repeated mistakes in documentation. That would be relatively easy to deal with through some training or general reminders to those involved in their production. The same applies if you are simply trying to come up with a new idea. However Innovation (which of course is closely associated with Creativity) will generally benefit from some degree of process to generate the ideas.

On the other hand there are the more complex problems that are in need of a solution. Some key things to consider are who is affected; how far-reaching those effects are; and who owns the problem. It is no use applying individual techniques to something that requires the involvement of multiple stakeholders, the answer (no matter how good) will not take hold due to lack of ownership. On top of all this we need to consider the styles and personal attributes of the players. If the predominant style is incremental change - then it is no good going down the route of techniques that are likely to result in step-change proposals.

As you can imagine - this all starts to get messy trying to configure an approach that will work with the resources that are available and which is appropriate to the problem under consideration. So here are a couple of flow charts that will help you to decide.

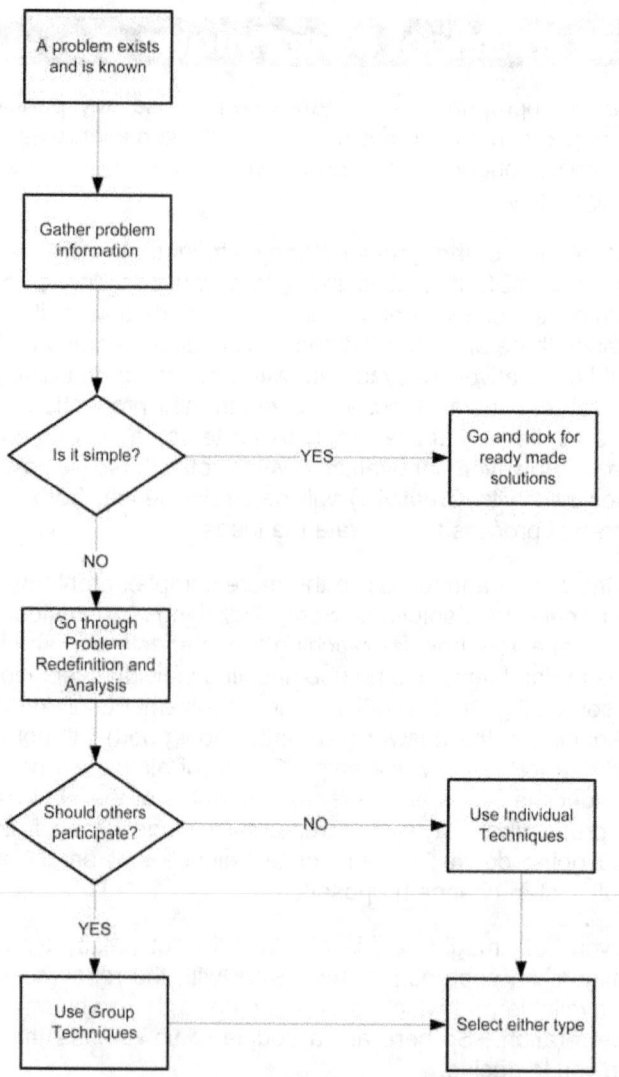

Figure 1 Selecting techniques for Problem Definition

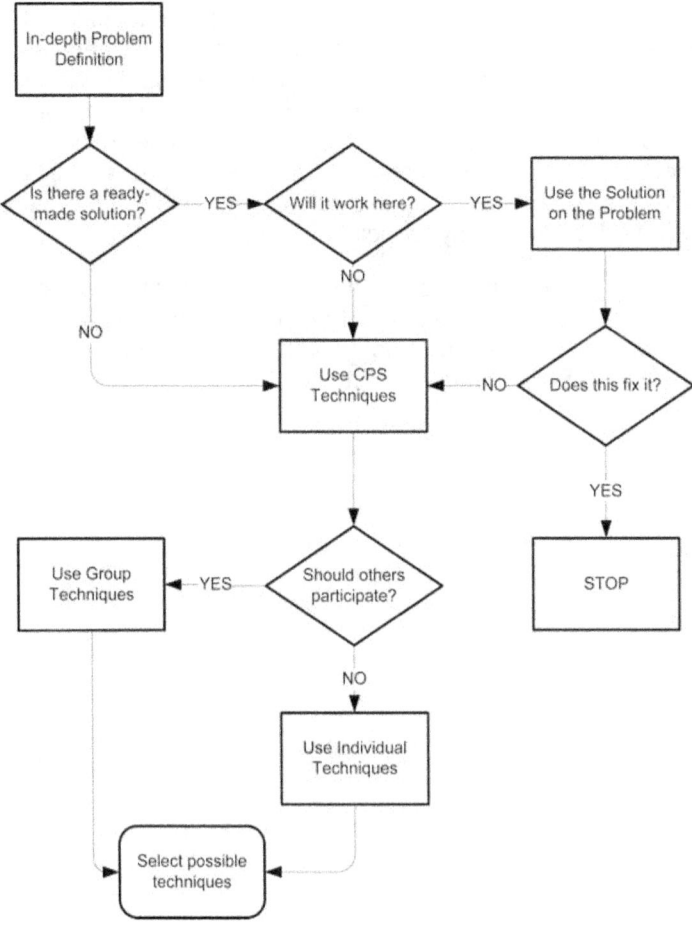

Figure 2 What sort of Idea Generation?

Once you have sorted out in either case whether you are going down the individual or group routes for analysis or idea generation everything becomes much easier to work out.

The governing factors are now more to do with personal style of the participants and, to some extent, how radical a solution might be required.

Very large scale techniques are seldom used unless the project itself is going to impact huge numbers of people or places. A case in point would be trying to evolve the solution for the route(s) of HS2 (the High Speed train network from London to the Midlands and the North). These tend to be more consultative in style with multiple iterations until an agreed solution can be found (or maybe which is the least worst - depending on your point of view).

We're not going to discuss these types of Idea Generation here other than to give a list of potential techniques that you could go and research if they look likely to be needed. See *Big Group Stuff* on page 117 et seq.

Understanding Creative Style

Like everything that humans do there are differences or preferences in our sub-conscious that impact how we engage. The reason for all this variation lies within our personal psychology. This drives the subtle variations in how we perceive the world and our preferences when interacting with others. You can study this elsewhere - it really can be quite fascinating.

Creativity has its own set of styles - each with a unique advantage but it's also dangerous to rely on just one source. As we shall see, the interaction of styles and communication are also very important. Creativity simply won't flourish if communications are constantly blocked or breaking down. This disruption can be as much to do with the psychological traits of individuals as it is with organisational structures and processes.

The clever people get to know their own preferred style and then practice operating with others. It's like changing your clothes according to the activity you are about to undertake. Hiking boots are no use on the squash court. Thick gloves don't help when writing an email. So even though you have a preferred dress style you also amend it according to what you are about to go and do (although I do admit to having done gardening in a suit).

However there is one key message. Understand that the differences exist, so try and get to know your own profile. Then look at how that might or might not fit with a balanced team. Once you know you can make allowances. You can also allow others to critique your style and how it helps or hinders. Don't be afraid - this is not a personal attack. Think more about how professional football teams realign their formation to allow certain skills to blend better. And then how the coach will re-jig that when up against specific opposition.

So what are these styles? Well the best way of describing them is to look at the opposing ways we deal with information and the world around us. Do we evaluate more than imagine? Do we jump right in to experience or do we pause to think about things?

In dealing with creativity people with different cognitive styles (for instance those measured by MBTI[5] or Kolb[6]) may bring different needs or preferences to the problem solving arena. This may affect the sorts of techniques that they prefer. Other personal choices may reflect familiarity with techniques or degrees of confidence in using them. What we are trying to do in this book is set out a number of varied options that are relatively easy to grasp - thereby making initial choices a lot simpler.

People with different styles are likely to prefer different stages of the CPS process. Consequently they are also likely to prefer techniques that are most associated with those stages. For instance we might expect that people who prefer to learn by direct experience (as described by Kolb) will operate best in a pilot environment. If they are in IT development they are likely to work with an Agile rather than a formal waterfall method.

> *The Agile Method is a particular approach to project management that is utilised in software development. This assists teams in responding to the unpredictability of constructing software and uses incremental, iterative work sequences that are commonly known as sprints.*

According to Dr Min Basadur[7], many people view admitting to having a problem that they can't solve as a weakness. There is also a tendency to find blame for the existence of a

---

[5] Myers-Briggs Type Indicator - a measure based on Jungian understanding of an individual's psychological preferences.

[6] Kolb's learning styles are defined by an individual's relative preference for the four modes of the learning cycle described in experiential learning theory: Concrete Experience, Reflective Observation, Abstract Conceptualization, and Active Experimentation.

[7] Min Basadur is Professor Emeritus of Innovation in the Michael G. DeGroote School of Business at McMaster University and Founder of Basadur Applied Creativity

problem – implying that it exists because of someone's failure to do the right thing.

> The Basadur Creative Problem Solving Profile (CPSP) Inventory which he devised measures an individual's unique blend of preferences for the four stages of the creative process. By plotting Inventory scores on a two dimensional graph, an individual can display his or her own preferred blend of the four different stages. The largest quadrant on the graph represents the individual's preferred or dominant style. The sizes of the other quadrants represent supporting orientations in turn.

It lists 4 types:

- **Generator** - gets things started
- **Conceptualiser** - puts ideas together
- **Optimiser** - turns abstract ideas into practical solutions
- **Implementer** - gets things done

If you want to get your own profile then you should visit **http://www.basadur.com** However even just being aware of its existence is probably enough to get you or your team thinking along the right lines.

Each unique style reflects the individual's preferences for ways of gaining and using knowledge. There are those who:

- understand by experiencing;
- understand through abstract thinking & analysis;
- use understanding to generate options;
- use understanding to evaluate options

As with all such inventories there is no one right answer or style that fits all situations. What is important as an executive charged with ensuring creativity can take hold is to recognise this and make appropriate allowances. Knowing your team and their stylistic preferences is a good foundation.

Think of it this way - we all know there are those who are good at fixing things like car engines, others who are a whizz with a spreadsheet. The two are not necessarily the same person and you will choose according to the circumstance who you want to do a job. Creativity is no different - just that we don't always know who has what preference.

Imagine you had to diagnose and fix a complex problem but had no idea of the relevant skills available. Wouldn't you want to involve a good mix of people in the hope that together they might crack it?

So try asking what sorts of things people are comfortable with. Then blend the results to get a good mix of approaches. After all what works best is diversity and understanding shared strengths and weaknesses is an important part of managing things. You help your organisation to become more creative simply by encouraging the diversity.

The enemy of creativity is Groupthink - where everyone is selected to a single model and nobody challenges the paradigm. It can often plague relatively small organisations with a strong founder. The propensity to select more people like you is strong; after all, the founder has set things going so must be right. Why wouldn't you want more of the same? Except, as we know, it is diversity that succeeds.

What kind of Creative Leader are you?

It's no good simply following a standard set of processes if you want to be effective at getting creativity working in your organisation. You need to understand what your natural style is and then work out strategies for that to encourage a good mix of all of them in your team(s). So first of all you need to find out what your own preferences are. How you naturally tackle creativity and all that it entails.

There is a very simple but at the same time quite insightful personality test based on visual shapes. Various groups and organisations list a version of this in their material (often claiming copyright in the process). However it was Susan

Dellinger who developed the idea as far back as 1978 and published a book[8] on the topic in 1989.

According to the Psycho-Geometrics® theory all you have to do is to look at the geometric shapes and choose the one that you think best represents you as a person. This is the shape that you can clearly identify yourself with.

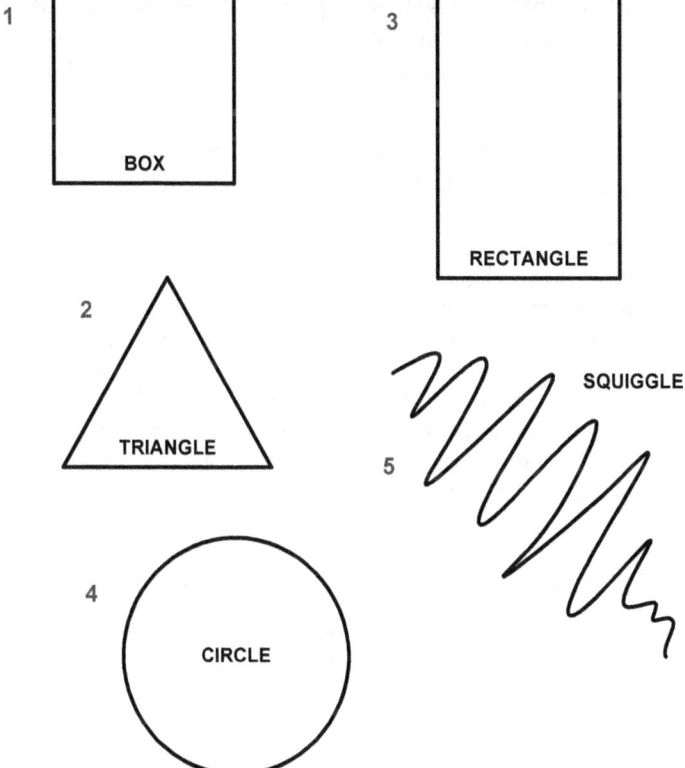

Then simply arrange the other shapes in order of preference. You are most likely to be a blend of the first two preferences

---

[8] Dellinger, S. (1989) **Psycho-Geometrics: How to Use Geometric Psychology to Influence People**, Prentice Hall

but you ought to try and see if you can recognise the other traits in people you know and work with.

The theory states that people who choose a linear shape (box, triangle, or rectangle) tend to be left-brain thinkers, taking a logical and organised approach to life.

Those who choose the circle or squiggle are categorised as a right-brain thinker. They tend to process information in a less linear and more configurable way. They are more interested in the whole rather than its individual parts. Right-brain thinkers place emphasis on creativity and intuition.

According to Dellinger preferences for the various shapes display distinct characteristics:

(1) Box:
A hard worker, diligent, perseveres and who always strives for completion. Patience and a methodical nature make them skilled specialists. A Box collects information and has it neatly organised on their shelves. They are able to quickly retrieve the desired facts. These are people who are characterised by logical thought and mathematical mindsets. They analyse and calculate answers to problems, rather than trusting instinct or inference. *"I did it!"*

They don't like the unexpected or surprises. Their ideal is a planned regular life where everything is predictable.

Positive Traits	**Negative Traits**
Organised	Meticulous
Detail Oriented	Anal Retentive
Knowledgeable	Procrastinating
Analytical	Cool, aloof
Persevering	Resistant to Change
Perfectionist	Loner
Patient	Complaining

Boxes find it stressful to deal with all the other types.

(2) Triangle:

Focused on the bottom line and driven by results. Triangles are good at focusing on goals and analysing situations. They want to be right in everything and find it difficult to admit their mistakes. *"You do it!"*

They can be very self-absorbed but can also be well-respected, sometimes feared by others. They are less interested in the work itself than their career. However they are good problem-solvers. They prefer working in small groups but interrupt and can be restless.

Also they can't imagine why anyone would want to be anything other than a Triangle! Apparently the Dutch think all Germans are Triangles whereas they see themselves as Circles. This kind of stereo-typing can contribute to real difficulties in communication. In turn that will disrupt attempts to deliver change.

Positive Traits	Negative Traits
Leader	Self-centred
Focused	Overloaded
Decisive	Dogmatic
Ambitious	Status-oriented
Competitive	Political
Athletic	Driven

Triangles find it stressful to deal with Squiggles, Rectangles and Circles.

(3) Rectangle:

These tend to be people in some kind of transition in their life. They are dissatisfied with their lives and are looking for chances to improve their circumstances. They are in a period of growth, change and searching. *"Why?"*

Their most significant features take the form of inconsistent and unpredictable behaviour, coupled with low self-esteem. However they often try to do things that have never been done and are open to new ideas and people.

Positive Traits	Negative Traits
Open-minded	Confused
Exciting	Low self-esteem
Searching	Inconsistent
Inquisitive	Gullible
Growing	Disingenuous
Courageous	Unpredictable

Rectangle types find it stressful to deal with Triangles, Squiggles and Boxes.

(4) Circle:

They will do whatever it takes to make co-workers, friends, and family happy. They stabilise the group and have a high capacity for sympathy and empathy. Peacemakers who avoid conflict or making unpopular decisions. On the other hand they may over-commit; taking on more than they can handle. The Circle really values people. *"No problem!"*

They are right-brain thinkers, not logical but creative and more emotionally charged. The processing of information in such people is not consistent and resembles a mosaic pattern. The main feature of their style of thinking is a focus on the subjective aspects of the problem.

Positive Traits	Negative Traits
Friendly	Over personal
Nurturing	Melancholy
Persuasive	Manipulative
Empathetic	Gossipy
Generous	Self-blaming
Stabilising	Apolitical
Reflective	Indecisive

Circles find it stressful to deal with Boxes and Triangles.

(5) Squiggle:

The Squiggle is a symbol of creativity and is the only one of the shapes that is not closed. They are more configurative when processing information - able to produce truly great and new ideas. They frequently challenge the status quo and are future oriented; more interested in possibilities than reality. ***"What if?"***

The Squiggle can not work in one place for a long time - this is, after all, boring and there are so many other interesting things to see and experience. They will need help in following through to complete things.

Positive Traits	Negative Traits
Creative	Disorganised
Conceptual	Impractical
Futuristic	Unrealistic
Intuitive	Illogical
Expressive	Eccentric
Motivating	Naïve
Witty/Sexy	Uninhibited

Squiggles find it stressful to deal with Boxes and Triangles.

There are a good number of slightly different interpretations of all this material. What's important is to understand that it generally seems to work as a predictor of how people will interact, their relative strengths and weaknesses. Do your own researches to get more information but remember **why** you need to know. It's about getting the right balance into the creativity of your team(s).

Hippies, artists, entrepreneurs, drops outs, dreamers and all kinds of creative thinkers are sometimes thought to lack the discipline to lead a responsible life. However, many of the perceived weaknesses of creative thinkers are actually strengths. Their ability to daydream and imagine the unheard of are what drives mankind forward. However they often need help to develop pragmatic solutions. It is a real team effort.

Cognitive Bias and Style

Why creativity isn't easy - your cognitive biases explained:

There is the tendency to believe what we have always believed rather than accepting things might be different. If you do nothing about it then you won't get very far. Leonardo da Vinci recognised this and noted that the first impression of a problem is normally biased towards your usual way of thinking. This is cognitive bias and you need to recognise it because it rears its ugly head every time.

Leonardo recommended looking at the problem in at least three different ways to gain better understanding. Here are a couple of examples to show what I mean.

Example #1

Some time ago I was leaving the apartment block and put my hand on the door plate of the main door. It was hot to the touch. An initial response was *"Oh - that's a fault with the electrics in the lock - the lock needs replacing"*.

Then I dug a little deeper. What was causing the electrical fault - maybe it was a loose connection? That led to a second idea that maybe the lock required reassembling. As described below this was an **analytical** response.

But wait a minute. What has made an enclosed connection come loose? Maybe that had a different cause. On examination it was clear that the door closing mechanism might be at fault. Every time the door shuts it does so with a bang and that might have shaken connections loose over time. So merely by challenging the initial view I ended up by getting the maintenance people to look at the door closer. This was a **relational** response (see below).

Example #2

Let's suppose that clients don't like using your customer service call centres. An immediate response may be that they simply need educating in how to get the best results. *"It's oh so simple once you get the hang of it."* (And, by the way, we save money by not having to employ so many staff.)

Stop right there. At whose expense is **your** organisation saving money? Surely there's a trade-off between charges and customer experience? Take high street bank closures as an example. The argument goes that it is easier for customers to do their own transactions online. That's all well and good when those are straightforward. But what about these circumstances?

- Some businesses want to deposit cash or get bags of coin. How much of their time is now wasted in longer journeys to a bank to do this basic piece of business? Who is paying for the inconvenience?

- Again, what about those organisations that need multiple authorities or signatures as part of their financial controls? I've yet to see an online banking app that lets a transaction be set up and then forwarded to someone else for countersignature. It is suggested that blockchain technology will solve this but we aren't there yet. So these organisations can't use e-payments at all. Instead they continue to use cheques which the banks dislike because it costs money and time to process them.

These are alternate ways of looking at the same problem and give remarkably different insights as to how it might be solved.

There's a concept of whole-brain creativity which combines the different styles and thinking processes. The earlier shapes analysis will give some insight into you and your team's preferences.

Here are four other ways of looking at this:
- Analytical
- Intuitive
- Operational
- Relational

Everybody is creative in some way. The ideal team doing anything needs some native creativity to keep on top of the challenges it faces.

Some different ways of encouraging this might be to have **ANALYTICAL** people use their strengths to synthesise information and describe opportunities. Use of **INTUITION** and imagination can lead to better insights and answers by envisioning future options. Meanwhile **OPERATIONAL** thinking can plan and mitigate risk in implementation. Finally a **RELATIONAL** dimension will give diverse perspectives and perhaps an overview of the impacts of what is proposed.

There has been some research that indicates the No.1 attribute sought by CEO's in their incoming workforce is Creativity. Now let's juxtapose that with how those same CEO's behave. If they are **not** embedding creativity in every aspect of the organisation then actions are going to speak louder than desire. It's like saying that you want to be fit and healthy - and then bingeing on fast food and not taking exercise.

Embedding Creativity is like having a good gym routine - the sort that tackles all the muscle groups not just running on a treadmill for half an hour three times a week. Now what kind of gym bunny are you? Be honest... Hopefully you get my drift. With Creativity you truly do have to walk the talk.

The big challenge is finding time to put all this into practice. Creativity requires space. This may also explain why meditation has been shown to increase creativity as well. Some people meditate so that they can let go of existing thoughts and patterns in their mind and make space for new ones. But not everyone wants to meditate. Lots of business people feel like they just can't take the time. So what else can you do to achieve the benefits of letting the mind wander?

Countering the bias

Neuroscience tells us that to stimulate creativity we need to break the routine. The brain evolved for efficiency and takes perceptual shortcuts, thereby saving energy. If we force the brain to break out of the habitual mould and re-categorise information we can get to really novel ways of thinking.

Of course it's not that simple. The brain (if it had a will) doesn't 'want' to operate like that so we have to do something to jolt it out of the groove. One side-effect of this 'groove tendency' is that even when presented with overwhelming facts, many people (including those who are highly educated) won't abandon their deeply held beliefs. Just think how many people insist on believing in Creation Theory irrespective of the evidence in favour of Darwinian Evolution. I know that's extreme but it **does** illustrate the point.

The antidote is personal experience. Firsthand seeing and experiencing of something shakes people up in ways that simple discussions and board-room debates can't. It's therefore extremely valuable to start creativity-building exercises or idea generation efforts outside the office. You need to confront the implicit or explicit assumptions of the participants.

> In **The Compleat Biz**[9] I made the point about how you can challenge preconceptions. My practical experience of doing this to MBA students was profound and long-lasting in its effect. They were challenged with seemingly impossible statements and relationships in a workshop environment. Constantly having their assumptions and assertions stood on their heads led to remarkable insights. Moreover it (to a greater or lesser extent) switched their brains ON to new ideas and ways of thinking.

I recently heard of the following sequence of events that occurred during the 2008 economic downturn. A global credit card retailer was looking for new-product ideas so they designed an exercise to stir up their thinking. Company leaders knew that consumer attitudes and behaviour had changed - 'credit' was now a dirty word and they needed to try something different. To find out which deeply held beliefs might be holding the company back, a team of their senior

---

[9] The Compleat Biz, Reroq Publishing (2009) ISBN 978-0-9561305-0-1

executives started to look for doctrinal conventions in the segmentation used across financial services. The models that they found generally consisted of mass-market, mass-affluent, and affluent customers.

It was apparent there were a number of assumptions at play that had not been challenged. For example the company had always behaved as if only its affluent customers cared deeply about travel-related card programmes. Or that only mass-market customers ever lived from payday to payday. The dominant view was that this group didn't have enough money to be interested in financial-planning products. Instead it was believed that only the wealthier customers would be likely to understand complex financial offerings.

This process of challenging beliefs identified a number of opportunities to be explored. These included simplifying products, creating new reward programmes, and working out novel attitudinal and behavioural segmentations to support new-product development.

Let's suppose you want to get creative with **your** product offering to improve your market position. You can begin by asking questions about customers, industry norms, and even business models - and then systematically challenge the answers. For example:

- What business are we in?
- What level of customer service do people expect?
- What would customers never be willing to pay for?
- What channel strategy is essential to us?

This will start to give you better ideas about your customer avatars (short descriptions of who they are and how they behave). The answers may well be different from the standard segments used in marketing. If you change your propositions accordingly then the result will likely be better penetration and sales.

Analogies are both powerful and quite straightforward. Just draft a list of questions like the ones below and use them as a starting point for discussion.

- How would Rapanui[10] redesign our supply chain?
- How would American Express design our customer loyalty program?
- How would Google manage our data?
- How might Lego engage with our consumers?
- How could Ryanair cut our costs?

Creating constraints

Another simple tactic you can use to encourage creativity is to impose artificial constraints. This will inject some much-needed pressure into an otherwise low-risk exercise.

Forceful constraints have an interesting impact. It is a bit like looking at *Assumption Reversals* (see page 81) to imagine how not to get something done. It seems rather counter-intuitive imposing constraints to trigger innovation. Yet it often takes some forcing mechanisms to stop would-be creative thinkers spinning their wheels or staying in their comfort zones.

Here are some examples your team can use. Most managers can easily imagine other ones tailored to their own situation. Start by asking participants to imagine a world where they must function with severe limits - maybe like these:

- You can only interact with your customers online.
- You can only serve one market segment.
- You have to offer your value proposition with a partner organisation.
- The price of your product is cut in half.
- Your largest channel disappears overnight.
- You have to move from B2C to B2B or vice versa.
- You have to charge a five-fold price premium for your product.

---

[10] Rapanui is an innovative clothing company based in the UK but with ethical sourcing and sustainability right across its supply chain.

More styles

Creativity isn't the preserve of the few. By immersing people in unexpected environments, confronting their ingrained concepts, using analogies, and challenging the organisation to overcome difficult constraints they will dramatically boost their creative output.

Here's another measure of Creative Styles. Have a look at the following lists of attributes and rank each from most like you to least like you. Are you a Forager or a Synthesiser at heart?

Foragers - these are people who love seeing opportunities in everything. They have a constant flow of ideas about the directions the organisation could take. On the other hand they really don't like the detail, so tend to initiate ideas but don't complete them - which can be annoying.

Explorers - people who are great with concepts, love brainstorming and coming up with unusual ideas as well as the big picture. On the other hand they really don't do detail.

Synthesizers - those who are essentially practical. They want everything to be absolutely correct and focused. As a consequence they can be thoroughly irritated by both the Foragers and Explorers who are still enjoying discussing and collecting their ideas.

Disseminators - are really good at getting buy-in and just want the job done. One consequence of this emphasis on completion and being able to move on might annoy all of the other types.

If you think these ways of talking about people sound familiar - that's probably because they are. Many organisations have used style inventories with similar labels to describe preferences. The Belbin Self-Perception Inventory[11] is quite

---

[11] Meredith Belbin, **Management Teams: why they succeed or fail**

common and lists ways in which people work to manage or complete tasks.

Other ways of looking at how people deal with change can be useful. The psychologist Dr Michael Kirton[12] devised an index that shows the preferred way in which people cope. At one extreme are High Adaptors - who move in tiny increments, polishing and improving as they go along. At the other end of the scale are the High Innovators - great at step change and often highly intuitive. Unfortunately they can be seen as abrasive and arrogant by their Adaptive brethren. In turn they view the Adaptors as slow to catch on to ideas. This leads to communication difficulties as explained in the chapter beginning on page 12.

Adaptors use what is given to solve problems by time-honoured techniques. Alternatively, innovators look beyond what is given to solve problems with the aid of innovative technologies. Kirton suggests that while adaptors prefer to do well within a given paradigm, innovators would rather do differently, thereby striving to transcend existing paradigms. Neither is 'right' but recognising the differences is a useful precursor to getting things moving more harmoniously.

There's also a lot to be said for disruption giving rise to some creative chaos. The trick is to identify what is missing and, as an executive, make sure the gap is plugged. There are ways of doing that informally for short bursts - such as the use of metaphorical hats that can get people to behave in ways that are alien to their norm. As you can imagine recognising something is missing doesn't mean you can instantly slot it back in. If you need playfulness and the people are naturally staid you have to change something - albeit temporarily - to get them into that role.

On the other hand you might want a powerful voice and none of the players is naturally that way inclined. As we shall see

---

[12] Michael Kirton devised the Adaption-Innovation Inventory to describe cognitive styles in problem-solving.

later - the technique of Super Heroes on page 109 is one way of adopting an alter-ego to good effect.

Here are a couple of case studies that highlight ways in which this has worked.

Case Study (1):

I remember once getting the Chief Engineer from MBDA (the aerospace defence company who design and build missiles) to sit through a presentation with a puppet of a monkey on his finger. He started being mischievous and challenging in ways that were completely alien to his normal engineering habit of evaluating everything in a rather arid manner. Everyone noticed the difference. He also enjoyed the experience and admitted it made him think differently about what we were doing. So much so that he didn't want to give it back afterwards!

Case Study (2):

On another occasion I was working with an Aussie - Patrick Kidd - when he was a Lieutenant Colonel with the British Army setting up the Joint Chemical, Biological, Radiological and Nuclear Regiment. This unique organisation had responsibility for detection and decontamination anywhere in the world, on land, for UK armed forces. They had an assortment of high-tech gear and specialists that could be deployed anywhere at virtually no notice.

I was helping his Officers and Senior NCOs to develop their creativity skills so that they were better able to address complex situations - especially when dealing with foreign cultures. Afterwards he commented that he would be checking that they had their issue of finger puppets at all times! Of course he was being light-hearted but Patrick went on to become Head of the Modernisation Branch of the Australian Army, then went to work as a consultant for Deloitte in Australia before being appointed as Chief Executive for the 2018 Invictus Games in Sydney.

> Would you have expected a soldier to be so playful? Almost certainly not but clearly it has worked wonders for his career and the organisations for which he has been responsible.

There are other factors that might be considered - including the interesting effects of gender balance on company boards. Overall this is a very complex picture, since although companies with at least 15% female board representation appear to be more successful that may be attributable to a number of factors.

Large organisations, which generally employ more women at every level, may simply be more profitable than smaller ones. On the other hand the presence of women in the boardroom may be indicative of a different underlying culture. It is possible that this culture is one of the reasons for more profitable behaviours rather than simply a gender bias.

A report published by Credit Suisse in 2016 showed that companies with at least one woman director received a better return on their investments compared with companies with all-male boardrooms.

More innovative companies are more likely to use their talent effectively, regardless of gender. It is also possible that some companies that are already doing well have moved further ahead because they could afford to focus more resources on diversity. As is constantly shown - diversity is essential to get things working well and is a recurrent theme when putting together teams to deal with Creativity and address problems.

As an aside, female board members appear to have more of a positive impact on their company's performance in countries where women have more equal rights and treatment overall. That tends to indicate that there is something about the underlying culture (of inclusion and respect) that is perhaps more important.

All this is food for thought as you look at your own organisation and how it deals with complex problems. Perhaps the best place to start is taking a critical look at the organisation's culture.

I've noticed that this tends to be superficial in many organisations. There is plenty of published stuff pointing out how inclusive and respectful the organisation wants to be. Contrast that with the behaviours in the office or elsewhere and you get a different set of values coming through. This blew up globally with various allegations of sexual mis-behaviour in a variety of work settings during late 2017 and is becoming ever more important.

I remember having lunch some years ago with a director and senior managers of a client and was inwardly appalled at the misogyny that came through in the banter. They simply didn't hear themselves speaking or recognise how much it contradicted the values to which they were allegedly signed-up. It wasn't a comfortable experience and I was the outsider, not a work-colleague. So underlying culture is something that needs to be properly understood - not pasted over the cracks with nice statements. In turn that may or may not be impeding your attempts to get people working better together on problems.

Problem Analysis

These techniques are all about getting a really good understanding of the problem you are tackling. Frequently people assume they know what is wrong and go with that. Big mistake! The nature of organisational problems is that they often have ill-defined boundaries and stretch into areas that at first are not apparent.

More to the point, the causes may be somewhere else entirely. So it is essential to spend time on getting this bit right. Whilst you do so, expect some criticism from above (and occasionally from below) to just get on with things. Stand your ground - you are doing absolutely the right thing to make sure that you know what it is you are trying to solve. After a couple of different interventions people will stop bitching because it will be evident that this time spent in analysis is saving vast amounts of wasted effort later on.

Validation - part 1

Before we begin let's deal with something that affects almost all decision-making.

This isn't so much a technique for Problem Analysis or Idea Generation, more as a way of validating what we think might be done. It's always a good thing to give whatever is being proposed a hard time before we embark on the execution phase. So let's deal with one of the things that often plagues change, it is something called confirmation bias.

Let's look at how this works. Assume that there are four cards that show information as follows:

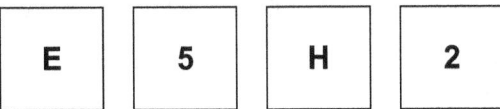

You are told that each card has a number on one side and a letter on the other. Which card(s) do you need to turn over to disprove the following statement?

"Any card with a consonant will have an even number on the other side."

What you need to do is disprove something. Human nature seeks confirmation that what they originally think is right. This confirmation bias often misdirects our efforts to doing the wrong things and therefore, given we are trying to implement the Right Solution to the Right Problem, it is essential we address the matter. So what do you think is the right answer? Jot it down.

We'll deal with the answers and what this means in Validation part 2 on page 68

Individual Analysis Techniques:

Art of Listening

There really is no substitute for listening to what people are telling you. As in the example in *Sharing* on page 62 it gives clarity to the situation.

You probably are used to getting feedback from others - it's something management at all levels seek on a regular basis. What they are less used to doing is to listen to the feedback and make it impersonal. Positive feedback is fine but merely tells you what you already thought. Negative feedback is hugely valuable provided you allow it as a learning exercise and don't get bogged down in the personal aspects. Take it, ingest it and act on it.

That has an interesting side-effect. Everyone gets to know they are being listened to and that it matters. They will start to come forward with more useful stuff that otherwise might lay buried. It's a great way of opening things up to allow in fresh air and get consensus on ways to move forward.

Checklists (for Problem Definition)
See fuller description of Checklists on page 83.

Comparative Customer
Being the comparative customer is a technique for validating what you are doing well and how others do better. It's not a creative way of solving a complex problem, more a way of encouraging continual experiment. The method goes as follows:

- Go through the process of purchasing your own product or service as a real consumer would. Record the experience, including photos if you can.

- Visit the stores or operations of other companies (including competitors) as a customer would and compare them with the same experiences at your own company.

- Conduct online research and gather information about one of your products or services (or those of a competitor) as any ordinary customer would. Try reaching out to your company with a specific product- or service-related question. Can your company answer it in a helpful and accessible way? FAQs are not the only answer - especially if they limit the subject matter and there is no ready way for the consumer to get more information.

- Observe and talk to real consumers in the places where they purchase and use your products to see what offerings accompany yours, what alternatives consumers consider, and how long they take to decide. In the digital environment tools can help. For instance on Amazon you will see prompts of what other buyers have purchased. LinkedIn will show you which other profiles people have been looking at, and so on.

Daydreaming

Allow the co-processor of your Right Brain to do some work and be assured that science is on your side.

A number of studies have shown that daydreaming is our brain in active problem-solving mode. So it's no bad thing to carry out activity that allows it the freedom to do just that. For different people that can vary. Some people take a long walk (not too strenuous) sufficient to take the mind off other things and meander where it will. I'm sure you know how that feels. Importantly work out what it is you are doing that allows your brain to get into that state.

Now you know what switch to use, take advantage of it. For one thing the brain, when we are daydreaming, isn't just working at the conscious level. Those daydreams are prompted from within and occasionally that is the sub-conscious processing a problem. Anything that allows your brain to work in the background while you are doing something mundane is good.

It is described by some people as working in low intensity cycles (cycling, driving or washing up are examples given). You may recall times when driving (for example) that you have suddenly cracked a problem. So daydreaming isn't a lightweight activity but can have really useful outcomes. One executive is reported as saying *"while ruminating on a given subject, it takes the pressure off the thought process and enables me to free-associate."* All it requires is some mental space.

Five W's and H (The Reporter's Notebook)

This is a very simple technique yet possibly the most-used one out there. These are six questions that any novice reporter on the local newspaper or radio station would be asking when interviewing someone. They get a good spread of information that builds a picture of what has happened. The five W's are: **WHO? WHAT? WHY? WHERE?** and **WHEN?** and they finish off with the question **HOW?**

Once you have got a good spread of answers on each of these questions the true nature of the problem will become much more apparent.

Armed only with these questions you can grill your Problem Owner and anyone else who has insight into the issues to get a better understanding of what is really causing the difficulties or needs to be changed. You can do this quite quickly, face-to-face or via phone or email. Just dig as much as you can to fill out the answers to each question.

Once you have your problem definition try reframing it (see below) and reading that back to the owner to see if they agree. It is also possible for a small group to use this technique, interviewing people who have knowledge of the situation. That has the extra benefit of building on the slightly differing interpretations you might expect when more than one person hears an answer.

Repeated WHY?

Much as the previous technique this is straightforward. However the delving is into each answer. *"Why is X a problem?"* will get a first answer. Follow that up with another *"Why does that matter/make a difference/cause more grief?"* Until you finally get to the bottom of it all. Some people don't like being asked repeated WHY? But that's where a little charm can work wonders up front. Make it clear that your only objective is to find out, not to lay blame.

Surprisingly many large organisations don't even go through these rudimentary approaches to define problems. Instead they assume and then search for a quick-fix solution. Predictably that means the solutions selected are generally to the wrong problem or don't address everything they should. Result - misery (as Mr Micawber was noted for saying).

Executives should be asking WHY? all the time. It reveals what is going on. More to the point they should encourage others to ask as well. I remember one Group Sales & Marketing Director who was leading a presentation to management and I started to ask a question by prefacing it with *"I know this may be a difficult question but I'm going to ask it anyway."* He responded that I always asked difficult questions - the board valued me for it - and then proceeded to actually address my concerns. So encouraging and valuing probing is a good thing. It develops trust and from time to time will get to the heart of issues before they get out of control.

Flipping the Binoculars

This technique leverages models from other industries and first surfaced at Salesforce.com Inc. They are an American cloud computing company based in San Francisco.

Method:
1. For example, if you're trying to increase customer loyalty, look at a company in a completely different industry. For instance if you are in engineering you might look at the John Lewis Partnership, and ask how it keeps customers coming back. Choose examples from an industry that is radically different from yours.

2. Get feedback from a range of different sources. While not everyone agrees, there is a good deal of research showing that diverse groups are more creative (that recurrent theme again!) In my own experience the organisations that succeed are prepared to look wider and be more varied in the teams they build. In so doing they bring together people from different backgrounds and perspectives. The ones that were really successful also took the time to talk to people from different industries to reframe their ideas.

Reflection on the process:
Oddly these are the sorts of conversations that, from time to time, happen at networking with bodies like the Institute of Directors. Yet how many company directors **actually** bother to talk outside an industry body or across disciplines? It tends to be the minority - which presupposes the rest have their heads in the proverbial sand to some extent. So the challenge for you is to do it more. It's really not that difficult to find someone from a different industry and ask for insight. More to the point it isn't a threatening activity either.

Evidence from the world of retailing is telling. Large businesses are having their models challenged by start-ups and disruptive approaches. The last few years have seen a catalogue of failures as household names have disappeared off the UK high street. Woolworths, BHS, Somerfield, Comet,

Netto, C&A, Littlewoods - all gone. Then there are those struggling to survive like Toys 'R' Us, Beales (department stores) MultiYork (furniture), Staples (office supplies), Greenwoods and Austin Reed (both menswear) or Jaeger (ladies fashion).

Jump-starting the Experience

This is useful to gain traction by swiping from another organisation or different industry to help transpose ideas or get insight into new concepts.

Essentially the idea is to get your people, in small groups, to go and have a look at how other organisations/businesses do things and from that to inspire ideas for change. For instance you might be looking to reinvent a proposition by improving customer experience. So send out teams to look at customer experience in a wide variety of places, from a chocolate boutique to major online retailers.

The outcome will be metaphor (again) that they need to translate back to your operations. There's no right or wrong way to Jump-start as long as you are prepared to look at some widely differing sources for inspiration. Creative swiping (as it is sometimes called) is a well-known technique and can cut out a lot of wasted time provided you think things through and don't overlook fundamental differences between the source and your own situation.

Many businesses do this to some extent when they perform a 'me too' implementation of product or service. However the more rigorous you are about it, the better the results and the greater chance of identifying some USP for your own version.

Magazine Rack

Another way of getting random stimulus is to go to the news stand and purchase three magazines that you would never buy in a million years. Like *Architectural Digest*, *Electronics Weekly*, *Pet Monthly*, that sort of thing.

Read them cover to cover and try to reframe the problem brief you are trying to crack with the target audience of those magazines in mind. This can not only be really good fun, but it will also open up new avenues of thought that can then be applied to the problem itself.

Mirroring

You can use this either to get further insight into the problem or to come up with ideas for its solution. It does (as the saying goes) exactly what it says on the tin. You look at the problem through a virtual mirror. What is Left is Right, what is Up is Down.

By examining things in this way you start to challenge what is going on. For instance, if something always operates as a process from Left to Right - then what happens if it goes the other way? Is that part of the problem or could it be part of the solution? Can you devise ways of making things happen in this world through the looking glass?

In Lewis Carroll's classic tale *"Through the Looking Glass"* whenever Alice tries to get to the top of the hill she ends up back where she started. Only when she decides to give up and go in the opposite direction does she suddenly find herself on top of the hill!

However you don't need mythical creatures to help you do this - even though a Harlequin Bat would not seem out of place in such a crazy universe.

Morphological Analysis

This is generally used for generating ideas to solve either two- or three-dimensional problems. You could use it for problems with many more dimensions but that gets very complex and we want to keep things simple. Therefore, if you look at your problem and can break it down into two or three dimensions this method can work well.

You will need some agreed criteria against which to measure the options generated.

Requirements:

It is a good idea to think ahead about the validation criteria you are going to apply. Otherwise you can do this exercise with pen and paper or maybe a spreadsheet to capture the dimensions and alternatives. A small group of contributors is ideal to bring out various aspects as everyone will see things slightly differently.

Method:

1. State the problem and its objectives.

2. Identify two or three major dimensions.

3. List the sub-divisions of each dimension.

4. Plot these onto a matrix (two-dimensions) or a cube (three-dimensions).

5. Select one sub-division from the first dimension and compare it with a sub-division from the other dimensions.

6. Evaluation - look at each combination to see what potential this may have for a solution to the problem. Some will be crazy, others mundane and one or two might be very interesting.

7. Discard those combinations that don't fit the objectives or that will be impractical to implement.

8. Using the agreed criteria, select the combination(s) that will be likely to solve the problem.

Example:

First let's look at a two-dimensional problem.

Consider a need to develop training across an organisation to cope with major new technology. That could be regarded as having components related to **level** (from individual to organisation) and across a variety of functional **areas** such as structure or process.

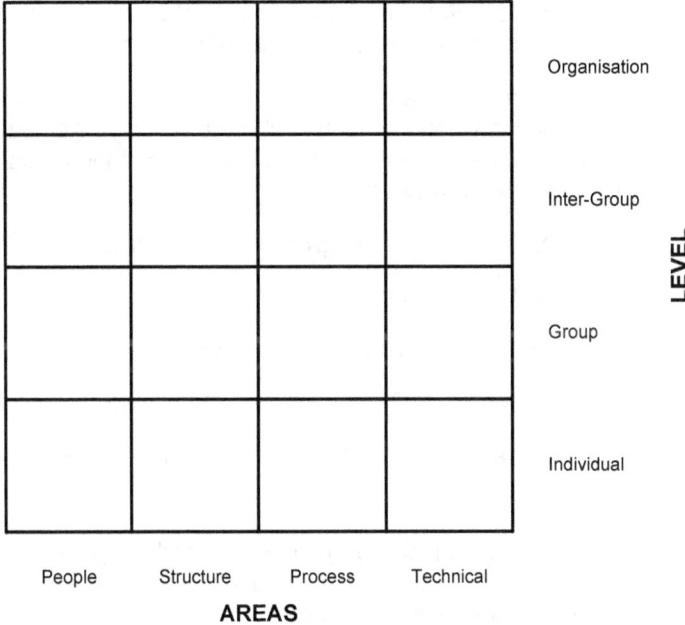

Figure 3 Two-dimensional analysis

This two-dimensional matrix produces 16 combinations of variable.

This might suggest a variety of programmes to deal with how to execute and deliver the training required to get the organisation ready for the technology change. For instance there might be some individual training around the process and technology. Group sessions on structure may be the answer if that needs to change. Certain individuals or teams may need some specific training on technology. Finally inter-group or organisational approaches to deal with changes in overall structure or processes to make sure the hand-offs are going to work in the operations.

Of course some things may be shown to be impractical or not cost-effective. Developing a technology approach to deliver the training might be very expensive, especially if that is to be organisation-wide. Reflect on how this might have worked for something that your organisation did in the past.

Now let's look at a three-dimensional model. Suppose we have developed a wealth of technical material or intellectual property and we want to work out how best to distribute this. We may have three broad areas:

Material	Target	Method
Instructions	Individual	Printed
FAQs	Teams	Online
Scenarios	Organisations	Masterclass
Investigation	Worldwide	Consultancy

Note - the Investigation will be looking in-depth at particular circumstances. This three-dimensional view is going to produce 64 combinations of variable

Instantly we can see that delivery via consultancy worldwide is not going to work for Instructions. On the other hand it may well be the solution for Investigations - provided it has an appropriate price-tag.

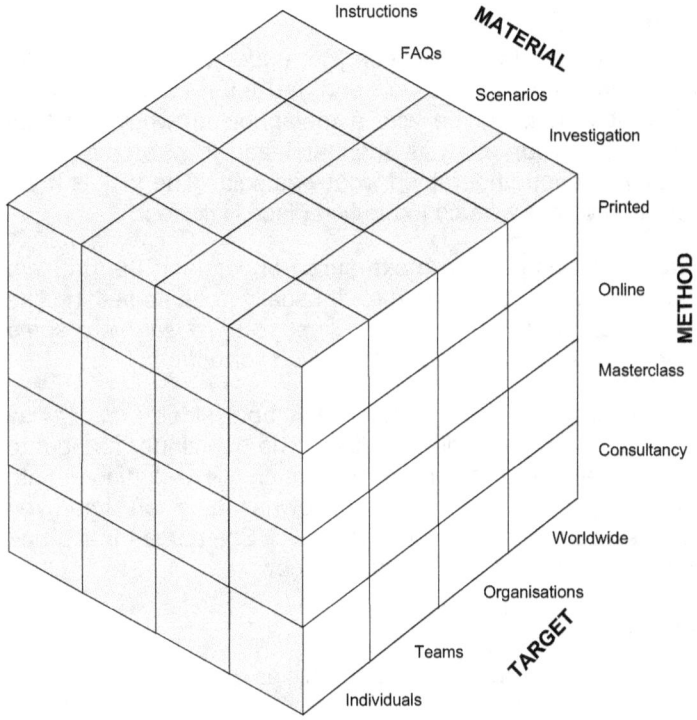

Figure 4 Three-dimensional analysis

Going further:

You can always synthesise from this basic model. For instance you might use it in reverse. Take a problem and split out a handful of options for dealing with it. For each option then provide alternate methods or mechanisms. Perhaps further refine that by even more options for each mechanism. As you filter out the impossibles at each stage you won't find the whole getting too cumbersome.

Methods for capturing the ideas will vary - from Post-It Notes to cards, online data entry and more. The mechanism is purely a matter of practicality. But also remember that occasionally it is good to walk away from it for a while and come back refreshed. That is more likely to lead to insight.

Reframing

It's a really good way to check your understanding. You take what someone has told you and you tell it back to them in different words, maybe with a metaphor thrown in. If they agree with your analysis then at least you can be pretty certain that you understood what was said. The trick is to be sure that what was said in the first place is correct.

I frequently use this to make sure I understand the problem that is being described to me. It usually goes something like this. *"Let me see if I can put what you just said into some other words to see if I understand you correctly ..."*

The other party never refuses and both sides come away with an enhanced understanding. The questioner has got to know what the problem is and often - by putting it into different words - the problem owner gets an improved understanding or way of looking at it. Sometimes that alone can lead to a solution looming into view.

Sharing

This is useful in opening up possibilities and new ventures.

Many people are worried that if they share a new business idea too broadly, someone else will run with it and they may lose the opportunity. Break out from that paradigm and when you have a promising business idea share it with every smart person you meet who has any interest in it. This will result in introductions and new information. Together that increases the likelihood that the idea will one day turn into a business.

I found this out when launching a new business based on a combination of skills and ideas surrounding change management. What was staring me in the face needed that reflection from someone to whom I was introduced. They recognised the USP of the proposition and pointed me in a slightly different direction to find an appropriate client base. The moment I started talking to the right people I suddenly found lots of interest and a willingness among them to talk to others in their networks about what I was offering.

Think Tech

Do some creative visualisations around how technology will impact your business at different points in the future. Make this a regular part of your organisation's processes. Who owns it? What authority will they have to push the output into actions? These are things the executive should make sure are happening.

When looking at business plans it is a common failing for people to assume that not much is going to change over the next few years. Instead it makes sense to get into the discipline of examining what the underlying technologies that affect your business will be a year from now. Extend that to two years from now, three years from now. You might even review the summary every six months.

You can look back over the last 3-5 five years and just see the huge changes that have occurred. The growth in use of Social Media is just one example. The world was very different and it's going to change even more, at an even quicker pace, in the years ahead.

Quantum leaps in technology will change the basis of forecasting. Make sure that you factor this in, using creative approaches to avoid cognitive bias along the way. Maybe each round of the forecasting should look at this from a different angle - reminiscent of applying the differing Creative Styles on page 37.

It may sound hackneyed but the growth of Information technology is phenomenal. It's not so long since a university computer cost £millions. Yet today people carry round technology that has massively more power and storage and yet is available for a few £'s per month. I recall being staggered at the first portable 1GB storage devices in the mid 1990s which had exchangeable cartridges not dissimilar in size to one of the old 8-track audio cartridges of the 1970s. Now I can put 2TB or more on a flash drive that fits in the palm of the hand for less than £10.

Unfamiliarity

Changing the paradigm can really help get you out of your comfort zone. Go and seek out unfamiliarity. Research shows that we are at our most creative when we are in an unfamiliar environment. One study showed that spending a few days out in nature disconnected from all devices, which is an unfamiliar and unusual experience for most people, led to a 50% increase in creativity.

On the other hand, if you don't have several days to retreat to the woods, how do you make time for new experiences? Actually the answer is probably already out there. The entire universe is filled with ideas and has in it what you are trying to create. By observing it you can take clues from everyday life by noticing every little thing and being inquisitive about the **how**, **why** and **what** of things around you.

My own preferred method is explained in the section on *Wynectics* (see page 110) forcing the brain into uncharted territory without me actually having to go anywhere.

Group Analysis Techniques:

Boundary Examination

This is a redefinitional technique. It is finding different ways of looking at the same material and helps to flesh out understanding of the problem under review. In this case the basis is in the boundaries that determine how information is organised. In turn those boundaries are usually based on assumptions. Neither the boundaries nor the assumptions are 'wrong'. Instead we are going to use them to find alternatives that may suggest insights.

Ill-structured problems tend to be open-ended and therefore their boundaries are not well defined at outset. During this process you are likely to redefine where they actually sit and understand why. The technique can be done solo but works much better with a group simply because someone is more likely to challenge assumptions.

Method:

1. Write down the initial problem statement.

2. Note any key words or phrases. You should then examine these for hidden assumptions. *(For instance you might say that the fault is in a machine on the factory floor - but doing so assumes it isn't something else.)*

3. Look at the assumptions suggested but don't question whether or not they are valid. Instead look for any important implications that are suggested. *(In our example that would imply that either the machinery is faulty or badly maintained - which widens the scope for cause of the problem.)*

4. Finally write down any new problem definition(s) suggested by those implications. *(Again, in our example, that might extend to maintenance scheduling or training.)*

The great thing about this technique is its ability to produce provocative definitions of the problem and clarify boundaries. In addition it really challenges those teams that have been too precise in their initial definition of the boundaries - a common problem when everyone is used to thinking the same way, as happens in organisations.

Sadly, in my experience, this technique is not used enough by organisations. If they did engage it would stop a lot of change setting off on shaky foundations.

Embrace Constraints

This technique works on the basis that creativity activates two different parts of the brain. The first being that part associated with daydreaming. The second works on administrative control. There is a useful connection between these two seemingly opposing concepts.

The ability to take free-flowing ideas and combine those with some management to produce something thoughtful is key. The constraints are not arbitrary limitations but connected to the underlying problem.

Here's an example. Suppose you are given an instruction to model a particular customer behaviour. There has to be a reason why this is needed. So that rationale is included with the instruction. Let's assume that the behaviour was linked to a particular type of purchase. But what happens if the product range changes (new technology, regulatory change or something else)? Is the modelling still required? So the knowledge of the expected outcome can inform whether to continue or do something else.

In the military, an objective may be set out for troops to seize. But suppose there is a massive counter attack? Or perhaps the enemy has suddenly retreated? Do they still execute the original tactics? Most unlikely - instead contingency kicks in or a pause is called while new plans are drawn up. And so it should be with the ideas you come up with. Set some constraints that make contextual sense, otherwise you might continue down the original path when the 'battle' has moved elsewhere.

For example, Rapanui (a cotton clothing manufacturer based on the Isle of Wight) wanted to combine ethical production, sustainability and - where possible - organic materials. There was a conundrum. Cotton takes a lot of water to grow and major effort to harvest. Bamboo, on the other hand is much more abundant, takes far less water or nutrients but is heavy on the processing. So they use both fibres in their clothing.

Then they wanted to reduce the impact of their factory in India - so built their own wind farm, thereby making sure the facility was energy sufficient.

Finally, when it comes to printing on T-shirts, they use organic inks and Direct To Garment technology. So they only produce what is ordered and there is no surplus stock. And to cap it all they actively encourage customers to recycle old garments by offering free returns and a £5 voucher when they are sent back. As a result they have a large following among ethical and environmentally conscious organisations.

You can be more drastic and produce constraints that go head to head. Do double the business with half the impact. Assume that material costs will double and market share will shrink - but we cannot abandon the market.

All these sorts of ideas create tensions and allowing people to work with them will help drive innovative solutions.

Fishbone Diagram

Sometimes called an Ishikawa Diagram (after its Japanese inventor Kaoru Ishikawa, who pioneered quality management processes in the Kawasaki shipyards) this can be used either as an individual or a group technique. It is listed here because it is often useful to do this with a small group who can challenge and add to the emerging diagram.

Essentially you start with a single spine with a head and tail. These give it a causal direction so you can start to break things down into components or ribs coming off the spine. Each component may have sub-causes which are shown as divisions on the ribs. The head represents the complete problem.

Taking the analysis down three or four levels is usually sufficient to get a good understanding of the causes of the problem and how they are related. Once you have this information it is often possible to identify ways to avoid some of the causes completely and see how to mitigate others.

The resulting diagram will look something like this, with labels on each of the branches. The problem illustrated here is a Faulty Product.

Some people are naturally very good at filling out these diagrams, often because they have comprehensive knowledge of the areas under consideration or, occasionally because they just have an intuitive ability to see what might be going on. If you are one of those people then you will find this an easy technique to do on your own.

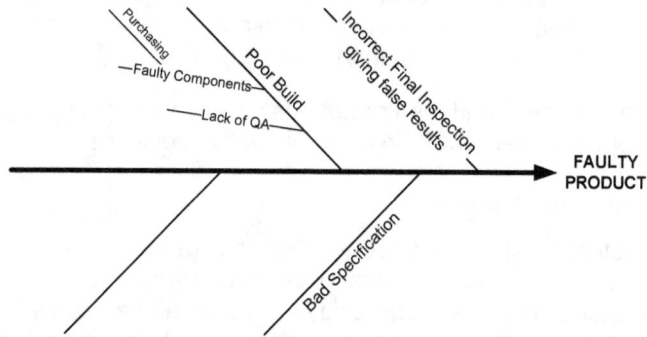

Figure 5 Ishikawa Diagram for Faulty Product

Kepner-Tregoe

This method was devised by Chuck Kepner[13] and Benjamin Tregoe[14] and today is still used worldwide by organisations and companies for decision making and problem solving.

It is included here simply because you might come across it or references to it all over the place. I've personally never felt the need to use it. However it would work best if carried out by a group rather than an individual.

It describes a 7-stage Problem Analysis Cycle as follows:

1. Identify Problem Areas

---

[13] Charles Higgins (Chuck) Kepner; (1922 - 2016) was a famous American problem solving expert. He also was a successful entrepreneur and management consultant, who helped hundreds of companies in sixty different countries. His work and methodologies on strategic thinking have been applied everywhere from NASA and the CIA to prominent organisations throughout the world.

[14] Benjamin Tregoe Jr. (1927-2005) was co-founder of Kepner-Tregoe, an international management consultancy, where he served as Chairman until his death in 2005.

2. Examine Problem Areas, establish priorities and select a problem

3. Determine the precise nature of the problem

4. Examine the Problem Specification (What Is and Is Not) and identify characteristics that distinguish between the two sides (the Problem Distinctions)

5. Examine the Problem Distinctions to determine relevant changes that might have caused the problem

6. From the Relevant Changes deduce Possible Causes

7. Finally test the Possible Causes to see to what extent they account for the What Is and Is Not Characteristics.

As you can see this is not a million miles away from the much simpler Divergence and Analysis phase at the beginning of our standard CPS Cycle. If you really want to use this level of rigour in your analysis then by all means go and research the method in much greater detail. It is certainly robust but incurs a degree of analytical overhead that, in my view, is way beyond what most problems require. Using our driving lesson analogy this is seriously advanced stuff on the skidpan.

Validation - part 2

So what was your answer to the question about which cards to turn over? (See page 49.)

The correct answer is **5 & H**. Why? Well we are trying to disprove the statement and therefore if **5** has a consonant on the reverse that disproves it. Also, if **H** has an odd number on the reverse that also disproves it. However we have no information about what might be on the reverse of a vowel (the **E**). Nor, for that matter, is there anything about what should be on the reverse of an even number (in this case the number **2**). It is confirmation bias to assume that the original statement was exclusive - ie that it applied to ALL cards - whereas the information provided was much more specific as to the combination of even numbers and consonants on the SAME card.

What this tells us is that we should be asking DISPROVING QUESTIONS more often. Such as: *"If I'm not right about my assumption, what might go differently?"* or *"What if this solution doesn't work the way we imagine? What then?"* or *"What if I'm NOT right about my reasoning as to the cause of the problem? What else might be going on?"*

When it comes to selecting people we often make up our minds about them from initial impression and then continue to look for data that backs that up. Instead we should be more critical and ask the *What If?* questions that might contradict our assumptions.

As you can see - this doesn't require particular Creativity Skills but when we use this critical reasoning we can tune the creativity outcomes for a better result. That is something that the executive who is overseeing CPS should insist on - irrespective or their personal style or preferences. If you did nothing else other than correct confirmation bias in decision-making the impact on your organisation would be terrific.

It's all about Metaphor

If there is a secret to understanding creativity then I think this is it. Metaphor is a really good way of thinking about things and seeing the world through a different lens.

Of course not everybody is fantastic at describing things with metaphors but we all use them to some degree. Moreover we are surrounded by them in the everyday - from news items or commentary, in advertising or conversations and throw-away remarks.

Who hasn't heard something described as being *"as much use as a chocolate fireguard"*? Or *"the best thing since sliced bread"*? So actually there is plenty of experience in our surroundings of ways to describe some attribute or other that gets an idea across succinctly.

That's why metaphor crops up time and again in creativity - whether that's in relation to describing attributes of a problem or ways of potentially seeing a solution. And metaphors aren't always written or verbal statements; they can also be visual or kinæsthetic. Imagine a picture of someone behind bars, hands grasping the cage trying to get out. It might be a visual metaphor for someone struggling to break free from constraint at work. In turn that constraint might not be physical but may be influence or organisational authority. Whatever the case, if you saw the picture when someone was trying to describe how they felt about the problem you would pretty quickly understand what they were trying to communicate.

An example of a physical (kinæsthetic) metaphor might actually be a rap on the knuckles or an arm round a shoulder. And the concept of heat, flashes of light or other attributes can have all sorts of useful connotations.

So when we are talking about problems and their potential solutions it pays to use metaphor. For one thing we start to see things in a slightly different light (note - that itself is a metaphor). The metaphor itself may suggest other similar or dissimilar things we might want to bring into the discussion,

If I tell you that I'm being dragged away from my desk by non-productive activity you might suggest I *"cut the rope"*. What that actually means would be context-dependent but it is one way of thinking about a solution. What is it precisely that is tying me to the distraction?

Many creativity techniques - especially in the arena of idea generation - don't produce direct answers. Instead what is suggested is a metaphor for the possible solution. It is highly unlikely that I'm actually roped up to non-productive activity but there is clearly some influence or connection that needs severing.

Secret (Confidential) Techniques:

There's occasionally a dichotomy for the senior executive who is trying to get to grips with a complex problem. Who else can they talk to if it involves confidential matters? Perhaps it involves someone senior who might be at the heart of it all.

I actually came across this when working on a very large project. Well to be precise it was 13 workstreams in a huge programme and things were just not ticking along as they should have been. The Programme Director asked me to come up with a solution to what he perceived as the problem - only he wasn't too sure exactly what was causing it.

Nonetheless something had to be done and I began thinking about it. After a short time I came to the conclusion that the Programme Manager, who was sitting diagonally opposite me at a bank of desks, was probably key in some way. So here's how the process worked that led to a resolution.

I knew that - whatever I thought - it couldn't be discussed openly. There were too many sensitivities and talking about the Programme Manager with one or more of her direct reports wasn't going to get me very far. So I decided to use a **Right Brain Drawing**.

What this allowed was for me to graphically reproduce my feelings about the issues in an abstract way. Using a sheet of plain A4 paper and a medium pencil I doodled for some time whilst thinking about the problem as I perceived it to be.

When I was convinced the 'picture' was as comprehensive as I could achieve, I approached a colleague at the next desk to see if he would help me. I told him that the 'picture' was an abstract about a problem I was trying to solve. I also told him that I couldn't tell him what it was. Nor was there a right way up to view it. I wanted him to look at it and suggest what he thought was 'wrong' with the representation and what his mind suggested might make it better. So I spun it onto his desk so it was not obvious which way to view it. Then all I had to do was listen and make notes. (Sometimes when interpreters turn it upside down relative to how it has been drawn they see things you never even thought of.)

Within 20 minutes I had a wealth of information - not least that where I thought the problem lay was correct because he identified issues of communication from the centre. It also gave some useful insights into how to fix it and at the end of the time he still didn't know what I was dealing with. To validate what I now knew I spun it at another colleague and was able to enrich my understanding even more.

That is what I call a really useful confidential technique. I could have spun it at a mate in the pub and got some insight without giving away any secrets. I rank it as one of the most creative sessions I ever had. The outcome was a confidential report to the Programme Director who made some personnel changes - including the removal of the Programme Manager's responsibility for planning the delivery of components. Within a couple of weeks the improvement in performance was noticed by everybody.

I've used this technique with individuals to get them to address confidential personal issues. I can give them feedback without ever knowing what the underlying issue is.

It invariably stuns them how perceptive I am - which just goes to show how powerful this type of communication can be.

Right Brain Drawing

This technique is based on the work of Betty Edwards[15] who was Professor of Art at California State and wanted to help people to learn how to draw. It turns out to be extremely useful in problem analysis - possibly one of the best techniques that I use personally when I get stuck.

The science:

Psychologists will tell you that all human beings are born with an innate ability to communicate that does not depend on verbal language. This is hardwired into our brains and is one reason why small babies smile when they see some things and frown or cry at others. The processing sits in a different part of the brain to normal language and is often referred to as Right Brain.

Within a few months this is overtaken by the acquisition of language - first by hearing and understanding and then eventually by talking. By the age of two years we tend to ignore the Right Brain communication but the capability is still there in everyone.

In order to connect with your own Right Brain you need to do two things.

- First take a plain sheet of paper and a medium pencil. Make sure it has a reasonable point - you might want to draw fine lines or dots as well as using it sideways to shade. The use of an HB pencil is also key as it will give

---

[15] Edwards, B. **Drawing on the Right Side of the Brain** Harper Collins, (1993); also **Drawing on the Artist Within** Harper Collins, (1995)

a variety of depths to the strokes depending on how hard you are pressing at any time.

- Second, sit and immerse yourself thinking about your problem and create an abstract doodle as you do so. This means you are not trying to draw a picture - just let your hands do their own thing with the pencil while you think. This is allowing your Right Brain to drive the communication and express the feelings onto the paper.

There are two rules to observe:

1. Don't draw anything real (houses, cars, money, people)
2. No words, letters or numbers.

The more of the paper you fill the better but don't worry too much if there are some blank bits, they are going to tell your interpreter something that you might not have realised.

Then you take your finished doodle to an interpreter. This is ideally someone you can talk with quite comfortably about things in general - that way they aren't going to feel too embarrassed about saying odd things about your drawing. They don't have to have any insight into the actual problem and it is often better that they have nothing to do with it at all.

They don't need any skill other than to be able to talk about what they see or what they think is missing. They cannot ask you questions and you simply listen to what they say and make notes. The whole thing is a visual metaphor for your problem and their feedback will, in turn, be a metaphor for the things that need addressing. Of course, since you have an understanding of the problem in the first place, it becomes quite easy for you to work out what that actually means needs to be done.

When they have finished - thank them but you don't have to reveal what you have been looking at. Of course if they have given you great insights then you can say so without letting on what they actually mean to you.

It's a huge advantage to be able to communicate using this alternative channel. For one thing it doesn't matter how well educated the other person is. Nor does it matter about their age, gender, native language or culture. As long as you can understand what they are saying in response to the visual stimulus from your drawing you are getting real feedback.

Occasionally, if language is a problem in this respect, I get the respondent to 'complete' the picture to make it whole according to how they view it. If you don't want to lose the original - then a photocopy will do for them to add their own doodling. You will understand the result without explanation.

Get feedback from several people and the picture gets even richer. They might cumulatively add to the doodle and each time you get more insight. Whatever they do, at each stage take a picture for reference - just in case they or a reviewer decides to add to it, to show how it can be completed.

For the record here's a copy of a Right Brain Drawing from a client. This was done whilst they were alone on a long train journey and is quite the most beautiful I ever encountered. It was dealing with a very traumatic situation and the train journey gave the time and space to concentrate without major distractions of colleagues, phone or email. The client gave it to me at a subsequent meeting and I was able to diagnose ways of making things better without knowing what they had been thinking about.

However, don't be put off if your drawings aren't so elegant the process still works even with quite simple pictures. The trick is to immerse yourself in thinking about the problem as you let your hands doodle.

Finally - there's a more colourful alternative that you can do using pastels. This may (or may not) help the drawer to express their inner feelings and sub-conscious in ways that simple pencil can't quite achieve. For what it's worth my experience with pencil is that the drawer either gets truly creative and produces a rich picture or they stall at a few simple lines. Colour does add to the richness and people find that stimulating.

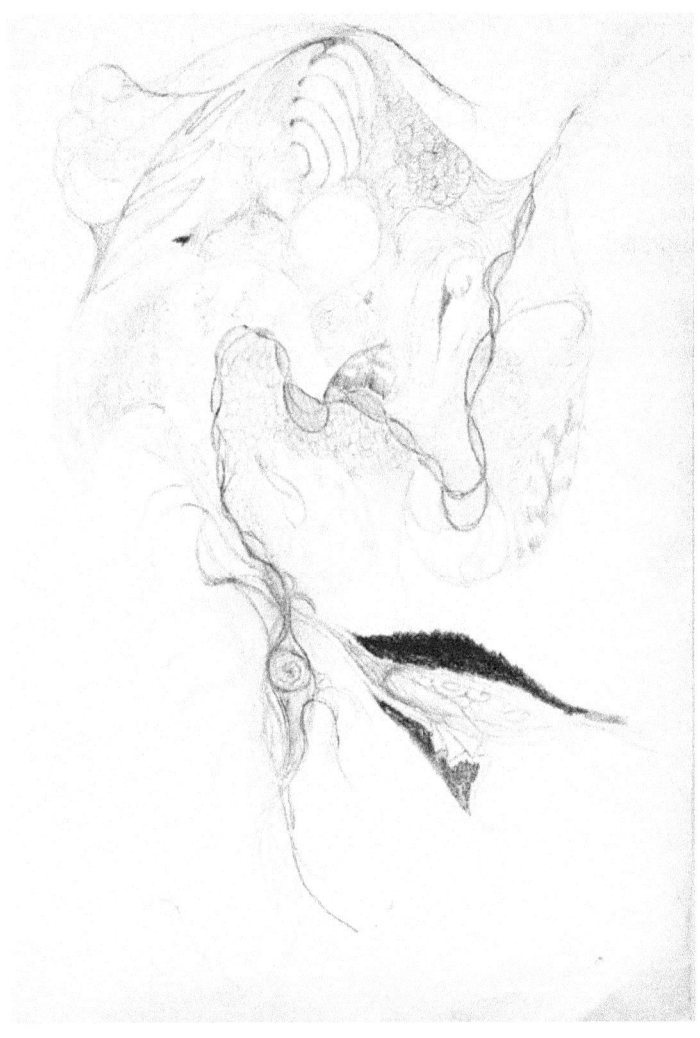

Figure 6 Client's Right Brain Drawing of a problem

In a slightly more colourful and messy version I've used flip-chart paper and finger paints. You can photograph the initial outcome using your phone and then get someone else to add their layer(s). Photos at each stage show the build up of a metaphorical solution and can be passed around for comment. This works quite well in a workshop environment and appeals to the playful side of some people. The photos are also easier to store for future reference. The only caveat is that colour blindness may interfere with how some people perceive what has been painted. On the other hand the same blindness may reveal things that normal vision doesn't see. It's all about being prepared to be open to the suggestions made.

Idea Generation

There are other books that give long lists of techniques you can use. The most comprehensive is Techniques of Structured Problem Solving[16] by Arthur B. Van Gundy Jr. but this can be quite expensive as it is now only readily available as a hardback print on demand edition. The problem with these compendiums of techniques is that very few of them are readily usable. It's all very well knowing about PICL[17] (for example) but it relies on you having the detailed resources it requires. In this case some 91 idea-stimulating questions organised into categories of **Who? What? Where? When?** and **Why?**

On the other hand there are also lots of online tools that suggest they can provide ideas - anything from plot-lines for a book, to social improvement. The problems with most - if not all - of these are that they are pre-populated either with strings of variables or are based on how someone else might have thought things through. De facto they don't necessarily get you anywhere truly original. On the other hand if you can find a Harlequin Bat or a Square Camel then you are definitely going to be out in new territory.

Finding a Harlequin Bat

Or indeed an Addictive Pig may well help when it comes to generating ideas for solving your problems. And no, I haven't lost my marbles. You see playfulness and getting right outside the paradigm are both key features of generating good ideas.

So in the following techniques you are going to see plenty of ways that take the participants some way from their comfort zones. In business people tend to think in groups. Anyone who has been with an organisation for more than 6 months

---

[16] ISBN 978 0442 288471

[17] Product Improvement Checklist - originally developed by Van Gundy for use with tangible products such as consumer goods.

will have got to understand what is expected and how the group behaves. As a result they are not generally going to challenge the norms and Groupthink takes hold.

That leads to everything being rooted in what is already known, rather than allowing in some fresh air. So going in search of a little craziness is actually the sane thing to do. And remember - **this stuff works** without the participants having to be some kind of super-mind.

Lateral Thinking

Most people will have heard of Edward de Bono and the concepts of Lateral Thinking. I'm not going to rework those here other than to point out that the purpose of Lateral Thinking is to disrupt the normal patterns of thinking to deliver new ways of envisaging the world. It's sometimes called thinking outside the box.

The detail of how it works and the frameworks it utilises are unknown to most people - even though almost everyone thinks they know what Lateral Thinking is.

As a consequence, if you really want to know more about it then I suggest doing your own researches and perhaps buying the de Bono book[18]. The benefits of becoming a Lateral Thinker are many - but, as mentioned at the beginning of this book, I'm not trying to make you be something you are not already. So for our purposes it is something to be aware of but not a core competence to enabling creativity from where you are right now. Oh, and by the way, there is something called Vertical Thinking as well.

---

[18] Lateral thinking: Creativity Step by Step ISBN13 9780241257548, Penguin Books (2016)

Individual Idea Generation Techniques:

Assumption Reversals

Technically this is a way of dealing with a logical paradox *"Aha"* - I hear you say *"what is one of those?"* Well they occur when a contradiction is perceived between the future and current states of a problem. For instance being required to improve output whilst cutting costs. Doing more with less is clearly some form of obstacle or hindrance to smooth progress.

Method:

Start by altering one or more of the underlying assumptions in a way that gives a more helpful view. This is an assumption reversal.

In our example that might mean reversing the assumption about reducing cost (for the time being).

1. List all the main assumptions, including any obvious ones that might otherwise be taken for granted.

2. Reverse each one in turn. There's no right answer to any of this so whatever they look like is fine.

3. Use these reversed assumptions as stimuli for idea generation.

This is similar to the *Reversals* technique (see page 90) but differs in that it is assumptions that are reversed, not the problem itself.

Attribute Listing

This technique has been around for a long time - probably because it is quite straightforward and doesn't require any special resources. It comprises three stages.

Method:
1. As with most methods, you start by stating the problem and its objectives.

2. Next break it down into its attributes. You do this by listing all the parts and characteristics of any product, idea or object related to the problem.

   Be careful not to get too hung-up about attributes that are not really essential to the problem. The suggestion is to focus on the primary functions.

3. The final step requires that you suspend any evaluation because in so doing you will allow some creative tensions or possible break-through ideas to surface.

   Then, whilst evaluation is not being allowed to intervene, systematically modify the attributes so that they meet the objectives of the problem.

Example:

Suppose you want to produce a better electric charger for a mobile device. Then we might see the following attributes:

- Plug into mains
- Power Cable
- Socket(s) for device cable
- Switch
- Connector cable
- High Impact Polystyrene moulded construction
- Rigid casing
- Transformer

Modification of those might result in the following:

- Runs off non-mains power
- Cordless
- Universal socket for any device
- Auto-sensing switch that cuts out when charging complete
- Adjacent charging
- Soft construction that can be remoulded to fit into something else
- Soft casing
- Solid state transformer

From these one could start to work on what the improved charger might look like and what its features might be.

Checklists

Although listed here under Idea Generation this could also be used to refine a problem definition. In that scenario it will help to focus the direction and ensure that areas haven't been overlooked.

It is most often used in Product Development, focusing on new uses for a product, idea or object.

The checklists themselves will vary and you will need to spend some time working out a reasonable list for your specific situation. However, here are a few ideas.

Physical Characteristics
- Size
- Shape
- Colour
- Material

Packaging Characteristics
- Insulation?
- Type of material
- Availability

Market
- Target consumer
- Competition
- Channels
- Distribution

Alternatively you might ask a series of questions, particularly if you are looking to develop from an existing product or proposition.

- What else is like this? Can that be adapted?
- Can the existing be modified?
- What can we take away?
- What can we add?

- How could this be reversed?
- Can the existing product be rearranged differently?
- What might we combine to make a new proposition?

You might consider compiling a checklist using SCAMPER (**S**ubstitute, **C**ombine, **A**dapt, **M**agnify/minimise, **P**ut to other use, **E**liminate/elaborate, and **R**earrange/reverse.)

Exaggerated Objectives

This is quite good fun and can be done by an individual or a group. The simple premise is that by exaggerating major problem objectives or criteria we can stimulate new ideas.

Method:

1. List the major objectives or requirements that a solution needs to meet.

2. Exaggerate these in any way possible. There is no right way - literally anything goes.

3. Each exaggeration is now a stimulus. Record whatever ideas this suggests. These ideas need not be related to the underlying objectives.

The fact that you have already specified problem objectives means that you have evaluation criteria against which to test the possible solutions. Just don't rush the process. Instead spend time on getting a good set of objectives up front.

There is an example overleaf.

Example:

Let's assume that a consulting business wants to attract more clients

Original Objectives	Exaggerated Objectives	Possible Solution
Reduce price	Increase prices x 10	- Offer premium service that is not offered by competitors
Uses highly qualified staff	No skills required for delivery	- Build an online platform that gives the answers - Get qualified people to write the material
Can operate at 90% capacity	Can operate at 1,000 x capacity	- Deliver online 1 : many automatically
No new premises needed	Be available worldwide	- Develop virtual consulting platform

Free Association

This is probably the simplest method that is most commonly used by people without realising it. It takes ideas from the mind's stream of consciousness. Compare it with other techniques that force some kind of relationship or constraint.

Its drawback is this lack of stimulus and, on the whole, I find it simply doesn't deliver anything like the quality or quantity of new ideas.

However it is something you can do. To give it a little more structure begin by starting with something that appears to be directly related to the problem. Then follow that by noting what this suggests (without trying to relate that to the problem at this stage).

You continue in this way until you ideally have at least 20 different associations. These can then be reviewed and you select the ones that appear to have the most relevance to the problem. If none of them work, then you can always go round the whole process with a different starting idea/object. As you can tell this method - even when structured - doesn't necessarily get the juices flowing. On the other hand a few people (and I really do mean **few**) are naturally gifted when it comes to plucking ideas out of thin air. That is one reason why classical brainstorming seldom works well. The *Wynectics* approach (page 110) knocks spots off these basic 'blue-sky' techniques.

Goal Reversal

Often, when considering a problem, the focus is on fixing it. But actually looking for ways to make it worse and then finding ways to prevent that happening can give more insight.

This is also similar to the *Reversals* technique (see page 90) but differs in that it is objectives that are reversed, not the problem itself.

I first came across this when I was using a basic software tool called *The Idea Generator*™ that was originally developed by Experience in Software Inc. It is long since disappeared as it was MS-DOS based. I caution you beware of other online tools calling themselves *The Idea Generator* - mostly they are nowhere near as good as they purport themselves to be.

So - what has Goal Reversal got to do with the original *Idea Generator*? Well the latter was a sequential process that captured data and then forced answers to questions. These were in turn used at later steps in the sequence.

Method:
1. First ask a set of questions around what are the goals you are trying to achieve.
2. The next step is to reverse each goal and look at what that might result in. So, for example, if the original goal was to reduce costs, then the reversal is to make them as high as possible.

3. Now look at ways of preventing that reverse goal. Sometimes this gives a different insight than merely trying to reach the original objective. For instance one way of making costs go up is to bespoke everything that you do. By contrast, NOT doing any bespoking will have the opposite effect. So if currently you are doing **some** bespoking then that should fall under the microscope as a candidate for cost-cutting.

Overall this reverse view will help to identify ways of reducing the problem as it exists. That in itself may be sufficient without having to go around a completely new development. Often it will also give you some alternate starting-points for looking at the definition and hence ideas for solution.

Metaphors

I include under this the idea of Analogy. The difference between the two really doesn't matter, since in either case they convey a meaning that is not literal.

Technically an analogy is a statement about how one thing is similar to another. *"Like a well-oiled machine"* is an example. Metaphor is a figure of speech that is not literally applicable to the subject in question. To make something *"cast in concrete"* indicates an immutability that is unrelated to a building site.

The point about all of these figures of speech is that we find them easier to understand as a shorthand way of expressing complex ideas. So often the ideas that come out of other techniques are not literal descriptions of what should happen next. We therefore need to start thinking a lot more in metaphor to allow these to be translated into reality.

There is often some fantasy element in a metaphor and many people find that alien to their thinking. The only way to overcome that reticence is practice. So, to coin yet another metaphor, get back on your bike.

There are formal ways of using metaphor that rely on some predetermined categories and a framework[19]. I don't ever use this and really don't see the point of this alternative - there are far better ways to get people thinking and the metaphors naturally fall out as a consequence.

Mirroring for idea generation

See technique on page 57.

NLP Techniques

There are whole libraries of books available on NLP and the methods it employs. Neuro-Linguistic Programming (NLP) is based on understanding that the neural pathways in the brain are not fixed. Various methods are used to either re-programme or to avoid some of the problems that are arising (personal issues). Also the techniques can help to deliver better communications, particularly where there is a conflict of perceptions (see below)

It was originally conceived and developed by John Grinder and Richard Bandler and began as a model of how we communicate and interact with ourselves and others. This NLP communication model explains how we process the information that comes in from outside us and what we do with it internally. The well-known hypnotist Paul McKenna now works alongside Dr. Bandler delivering NLP training for life skills. There is a large element of hynoptic technique involved in some NLP interventions.

In NLP there is the belief that 'the map is not the territory'. The internal representations that we make about an outside event are not essentially the event itself. What happens is that there is an external event and we run that event through our internal processing. We make an Internal Representation of that event. The Internal Representation of the event then combines with a physiology to create a state.

---

[19] Jensen, J.V. Metaphorical Constructs for the Problem-Solving Process - *Journal of Creative Behavior* (1975)

The word 'state' refers to the internal emotional state of the individual - whether they are happy, sad, motivated and so forth.

You may notice that other people treat their perceptions differently. Some people have to 'see' certain relationships between things, where others have to have it explained so they can 'hear it'. Still others have to 'get a grasp or a feeling' for the relationships. This is the essence of the NLP Communication Model.

Practitioners can facilitate all sorts of change in people - whether individually or in groups and occasionally this kind of intervention can be really helpful in problem solving. It is essentially a therapeutic method of effecting change and is listed here as an individual technique because that is predominantly how it is used.

Knowing and understanding how we receive and then filter information is a crucial element of NLP. In particular knowing how someone else is going to filter that same information can help to predict how they are going to react. Hence its usefulness in managing relationships and change.

That said there are a whole host of NLP techniques that are available so this isn't really a single technique but rather a different way of dealing with issues. I have used some NLP techniques to change perceptions and they do work. However there can also be a lot of hype about NLP and how it can solve so many things. Good practitioners have spent a lot of time in gaining qualification (often at considerable expense) and, as with anything that might be regarded as 'head bending', improper or unskilled use can be dangerous. It is good but it is not a panacea.

Private Brainstorming

This is, as the name indicates, a technique for the individual. No need for a facilitator, just pen and pad to note your ideas. However it is as well to try and follow the Rules for Brainstorming (see page 95). Putting down what comes into your head without trying to justify why it popped into your conscious.

You can take this a stage further and get a few people to do it on the same problem and then compare notes afterwards. Doing so would be a case of synthesis in action - modifying the technique to get a better or richer outcome. This would also convert it to a Nominal Group Technique.

Reversals

This is a way of gaining a different insight into the problem statement. Sometimes the statement as it stands can limit the ability for people to generate ideas and therefore by looking at this in an alternate light can help. This is a low-cost exercise but has varying degrees of success depending on the nature of the problem. See also *Goal Reversals* on page 86.

Method:

Because the meaning or order of the words used may not stimulate or promote unique ideas, we are going to change them. New perspectives can evolve by reversing the direction of a problem.

1. State the problem as defined.

2. Reverse the direction in any way possible. (Most important is to rearrange the information about the situation.)

3. State the new definition and examine that for practical implications.

4. If practical solutions are not forthcoming, then try a different way of reversing the problem until a satisfactory solution is produced.

Example:

In marketing it is frequently the case that an organisation is trying to find new customers. However what if that is turned round to say *"how can new customers come to us?"*

Traditionally finding new customers involves advertising the product or service. On the other hand finding customers who are looking for a product or service reverses the direction. We see this being fulfilled by websites that allow people to search for a tradesman or supplier. That came about because of a reversal and the launch of mechanisms to allow the advertising to flow in the reverse direction.

Self-hypnosis technique for problem solving

This will give your mind chance to process problems subconsciously and is used by creative thinkers to generate options and ideas.

1. **Find a Comfortable Position** - Get a position that you will be able to maintain easily for the time you are going to be doing this process. It can be sitting or lying down, though sitting is recommended to prevent you from falling asleep. Get yourself centred, just looking in front of you and breathing slowly and easily. Let yourself relax.

2. **Time** - Determine the length of time that you intend to spend and make a statement to **yourself** about it such as *"I am going into self hypnosis for 20 minutes... "* (or however long you want) You will be delighted to discover how well your 'internal clock' can keep track of the time for you.

3. **Purpose** - Make a second statement to yourself about your purpose in going into self-hypnosis. In this process, we allow the unconscious mind to work on the issue rather than giving suggestions throughout, so our purpose statement should reflect that fact. Here's how I say it: *"... for the purpose of allowing my unconscious mind to make the adjustments that are appropriate to assist me in ...   ."* Filling in the blank with what you want to achieve such as *"developing more confidence in social situations"*. I know that the text is 'wordy' but the actual words aren't nearly as important as the fact your statement acknowledges that you are turning this process over to your unconscious mind.

Exit State - Make a final statement to yourself about the state that you want to be in when you complete the process. Typically in hypnosis, we have heard the idea that you should come back feeling 'wide awake, alert and refreshed', but in the real world that may not be what you want. For example, if you are doing your self-hypnosis before bedtime, you may prefer to come out of it 'relaxed and ready for sleep'. If you're doing it before some project you may want to come out 'motivated and full of energy'. Simply say to yourself, "... *and when I'm finished, I'm going to feel ...*   ".

4. **The Process** - The following diagram can assist you with this.

   Looking in front of you, notice three things (one at a time) that you see. Go slowly, pausing for a moment on each. It is preferable that they be small things, such as a spot on the wall, a doorknob, the corner of a picture frame. Some people like to name the items as they look at them - *"I see the hinge on the door frame"*. (If you don't know the name for the thing, try *"I see that thing over there."*) These three visual references are represented in the diagram by the 3 V's (Visual) in the top line.

   Now turn your attention to your auditory channel and notice, one by one, three things that you hear. (You will notice that this allows you to incorporate sounds that *occur in the environment rather than being distracted by them.*) This is represented by the 3 A's (Auditory) on the diagram.

   Next, attend to your feeling and notice three sensations that you can feel. Again, go slowly from one to the next. It's useful to use sensations that normally are outside of your awareness, such as the weight of your spectacles, the feeling of your wristwatch, the texture of your shirt. This is represented by the 3 K's (Kinæsthetic) on the diagram.

   Continue the process using two Visuals, then two Auditories and then two Kinæsthetics.

In the same manner, continue (slowly) with one of each.

At this point you have completed the 'external' portion of the process. Now it's time to begin the 'internal' part.

Close your eyes.

Bring an image into your mind. Don't work too hard at this. You can construct an image or simply take what comes. It may be a point of light, it may be a beautiful beach or it could just be a pizza. If something comes to you just use it. If nothing comes, feel free to 'put something there'. Name it as you did above. This is the first V on the 'internal' side of the diagram. (I tend to see a variety of things - each time different.)

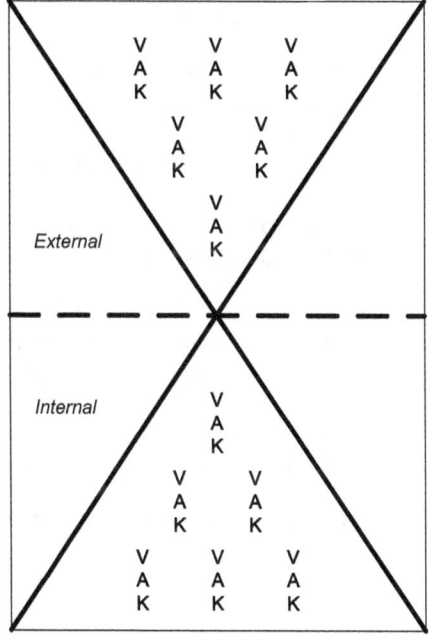

Pause and let a sound come into your awareness or generate one and name it. Although this is technically the internal part, if you should hear a sound outside or in the room with you, it's OK to use that. Remember that the idea is to incorporate things that you experience rather than being distracted by them. This is represented by the first A on the internal side of the diagram.

Next, become aware of a feeling and name it. It's preferable to do this internally - use your imagination. (Such as - I feel the warmth of the summer sun on my arms.) However, as with the auditory, if you actually have a physical sensation that gets your attention, use that. This is the first K on the internal side of the diagram.

Repeat the process with two images, then two sounds, then two feelings.

Repeat the cycle once again using three images, three sounds, and three feelings.

5. **Completing the Process** - It is not unusual **to** 'space out' or lose consciousness during the process. At first some people think that they've fallen asleep. But generally you will find yourself coming back automatically at the end of the allotted time. This is an indication that you weren't sleeping and that your unconscious mind was doing what you asked of it.

Note: Most people don't get all the way through the process. That's perfectly all right. If you complete the process before the time has ended, just continue with 4 images, sounds, feelings, then 5 and so on. As for your goals, trust that your unconscious mind is working for you in the background while you're doing the process.

Regular practice will yield better and better results.

Group Idea Generation Techniques:

Brainstorming

Everybody has heard about brainstorming. Most people even think they know how to do it ...!

Let's stop right there. I've never come across a group in any organisation that was much good at this before we got going together. Why? Because most folks think it's about tossing out ideas. But where is the stimulus - particularly after lunch? What usually results is a modest amount of ideas that are not very searching or creative. There is frequently a lot of talking across each other that doesn't help things along.

Also there is evidence from some quarters that Brainstorming simply doesn't actually work. I suspect this has a lot to do with the failure to facilitate properly and, more to the point, not using random stimuli or other prompts to get the ideas flowing. However it is important to understand **how** to brainstorm properly before bringing in those other elements.

So this section deals with what an executive needs to know about Brainstorming, how it is best done and how to ensure that actually happens.

Requirements:

An ideal group size is 6-12 people. They will need the following equipment:

- Whiteboard (the bigger the better)
- Flip-charts (I prefer to use two)
- Post-It Notes
- Marker Pens - enough for everyone
- Camera - useful to capture the data once it is all on the board(s) *(I've used a digital camera, Polaroid, video stills and a mobile phone - so this is easy)*

You also need to nominate the following roles:

Problem Owner
Facilitator (**Note:** they can **never** be the Problem Owner)
Scribe (although as you will see - this could be a shared responsibility)

Method:

1. First establish who the Problem Owner is. This is likely to be someone senior and you might want them to open the brainstorm with a few words about the importance of why the answers are needed. They can also answer any questions about the Problem Definition to ensure clarity.

2. Then let them leave the room - often this doesn't happen but it should. It gives the group the opportunity to be more radical without feeling they might be criticised. It will also stop the Problem Owner from butting in with a preferred solution before the process has had chance to work through.

3. Put up the Problem Statement where it can be seen before the brainstorm gets going.

There are also some rules that should be followed every time. There's a reason for this - it instils rigour into the process and can prevent the ideas getting side-tracked.

- Next the Facilitator will run through these **Rules for Brainstorming** which go as follows:

    o No justification is required for an idea - it simply gets captured

    o Build up - don't knock down - *which means that a new idea might build on something that's already out there in the room and doesn't have to link directly to the problem.*

    o Make sure all ideas get captured - *in practice the best way for this is to give everyone some Post-Its and a marker pen so they can write down their comments as they speak out. They then pass the* notes up to the front. That makes it easier for the Facilitator to collect everything in and stick it up on the boards. Duplicates will get dealt with later - better that than miss something off. Otherwise you have an appointed Scribe who is writing on the boards in response to what is being shouted out.

Note: Post-It Notes work better than writing on a board because afterwards you can move them around and put them into clusters to get more insight.

- Make the comments legible so that they can be seen from across the room

The Facilitator's role is to ensure that **all** the ideas expressed are captured; and to defuse any flare-ups or validation during the generation process. It is **not** their responsibility to come up with the ideas although most facilitators can and do contribute.

- Once the ideas have been generated you are likely to do a couple of things.
  - Cluster the results to see what the groupings suggest as possible actions or solutions
  - Perhaps do some voting to establish which of these the group thinks are most appropriate given the resources available.
- At this point invite the Problem Owner back and give them a brief summary of what has been suggested. They may elect one or more options for further investigation.

If you want your team(s) to be effective at Brainstorming then it is up to you to ensure that these guidelines are known and are being followed. The benefit in terms of quality and quantity of ideas they will generate as a result is well worth the rigour. Even a quick meeting where a team decides to brainstorm for a few minutes should follow the rules.

Reverse Brainstorming

This operates by trying to find reasons why things won't work. It's sometimes referred to as negative creativity or the tear-down method. However it can also be used to evaluate the proposed solutions from other methods.

Requirements:

6-12 people; a list of ideas to be considered

Method:

1. The objective of the session and the brainstorming rules are reviewed.

2. Ideas to be evaluated are displayed.

3. Individuals raise their hand or use some other mechanism to be recognised by the facilitator. They then offer a criticism of the first idea on the list.

4. Criticism continues until the first idea is exhausted and then moves to the next, and so on.

5. The group then examines the weaknesses that have been identified to see if they can generate possible solutions.

6. Ultimately one or more ideas will be shown to have the fewest number of weaknesses and be most likely to solve the problem. They become the prime candidate(s) for implementation.

Brainwriting

There are three variants that I am going to illustrate here. First is straightforward Brainwriting. Ideally this is done in a group although arguably you could do it solo with some gaps to allow yourself time to think of other things. It should take around 40 minutes to complete.

Requirements:

6 people, each with a sheet of paper and pen, sitting round a large table.

Method:

1. Facilitator or leader describes the problem.

2. Each person writes down three ideas in five minutes on their sheet of paper. In subsequent rounds these ideas may build on what is on the sheet in front of them.

3. Papers are passed one place around the table and the process is repeated. To give more psychological distance between people you might have an agreed pattern that is not quite so simple.

4. This repeats until everyone has their starting paper back (6 rounds). Ideas are then collected to be developed and sorted in any way you like.

The first variant is to place some constraints on the ideas that might be submitted. This allows you to keep the focus on a particular area or theme. To do this, the participants are given a sheet which already has some starter ideas on it and they can only build from those.

It is possible to keep a pool of these ideas so that future Brainwriting sessions can be kick-started.

The final variant is a game where the most improbable idea is awarded as winner.

Method:

1. After the problem has been read, Group members can *buy*[20] a specified number of blank, numbered cards from the facilitator. Record is made of the initials of each

---

[20] They might purchase them for a modest amount of money that becomes the prize. It is up to the facilitator to work out a suitable reward mechanism.

person on a separate sheet with all their card numbers so that the cards remain anonymous.

2. One idea is written per card.
3. The cards are displayed for the group to review and comment.
4. Participants individually study the ideas and try and convert them into a practical idea - the aim being that if one can be made practical, it is not improbable enough and will reduce the chances it can win. This is done in SILENCE but by writing on the card(s).
5. After 20 minutes the group moves to a voting phase. Each person having two votes to cast in favour of the two most improbable ideas. The person whose initials are recorded against the card with the most votes is the winner.
6. Now the pack of cards is split into two piles and each given to half the group. These sub-groups are then given time to discuss their half and come up with 6 practical solutions.
7. Finally each sub-group tries to sell its best ideas to the other. Together the whole group then tries to agree on a final list of the best ideas.

Comment:

The extent to which it is going to be effective will rely to a large extent on the facilitator who is conducting this chamber group through the suite in any of the variants.

The science:

This is a combination of some right brain processing (as people are looking either for practicalities or to come up with crazy ideas in the first place) and random stimulus. The brain is prompting ideas from within, having taken in the stimulus and processed that against the problem statement or objectives

The not quite random stimuli are the ideas that are already on the sheets or cards. Overall it is a relatively simple way of getting the combination working without having to rely on more radical stimuli.

Crawford Slip Writing

This is another brainwriting technique and was developed by C.C. Crawford[21] in the 1920s. Originally this used slips of paper to generate ideas. It is suitable for very large groups of participants and could readily be adapted using an intranet or messaging board.

Requirements:
- One pad of at least 25 slips of paper or large Post-It Notes (if using paper) for every participant
- There is no upper limit on the size of group
- Problem statement
- Evaluation task force

Method:
1. Problem statement is read out

2. Each person in the group (up to 5,000 people has been known) is instructed to begin writing one idea on each slip of paper. They should not worry about priority or importance.

3. After 5-10 minutes the group is instructed to stop writing. However in an electronic version this window might be kept open so that people could respond over a limited period of time at their convenience.

---

[21] Dr. C.C. Crawford - School of Public Administration, University of Southern California

4. The slips are collected.

5. The evaluation task force members evaluate the ideas by sorting them according to their frequency of occurrence or degree of usability.

6. The best ideas are then developed to proposals.

Benefits:

This generates a huge number of ideas in a very short timeframe. 90% of participants are likely to list 5 or more ideas in less than 10 minutes. Sorting the ideas into categories immediately after generation also speeds up the action planning.

In addition logistics are not usually an issue. Any meeting room(s) can be used irrespective of fixed or movable seating. Group participation is maximised and involvement has the normal effect of gaining more commitment to implementing the ideas.

Drawbacks:

In very large groups the effort to sort the ideas can be massive. There is therefore a temptation for the evaluation task force to be superficial in their assessment in order to give quick feedback to the group. It requires careful consideration as to whether to feedback on immediately obvious clear-cut groupings; and to defer the detail until analysis can be properly completed.

It also relies on individual ideation and therefore synergies between participants are effectively lost.

Doing the exercise over an extended time period using electronic methods leaves it open to collaboration or possible collusion between group members.

Human Sculpture

One of the things we cannot generally do when envisaging a problem is to ask an organisation how it feels. Especially if that organisation is not our own but may be a client or supplier. This technique can overcome that difficulty and finds a way of surfacing emotions. As such it is a great aid to Emotional Intelligence on the part of the problem-solving team. It can also deal with stakeholders that are relatively massive in numbers - all with a cast of only 8-12 people.

There are some caveats about how and when you might use this technique.

1. It requires the whole group to commit to supporting each other without judgement.

2. It can (and often does) reveal emotions and feelings that are both strong and unexpected. If this happens there has to be unconditional support from everyone for the person who exhibits them.

3. The facilitator needs to be comfortable dealing with these kinds of issues and be suitably trained or equipped if the subject matter is personal rather than organisational.

Examples of problems this is good for:

- Working out how teams might be affected by a corporate relocation
- Changing processes that involve suppliers or customers
- Dealing with tensions between personal life and organisational demands (for instance a manager being asked to work away from home for a long period to execute a major project)
- Modelling major change across borders (where it might otherwise be impossible to work out what the impacts are going to be in Mexico or Madrid)

Requirements:
- A well-defined problem
- Problem Owner who will actively participate

- Facilitator
- A group of players - ideally 6-10 to engage initially and a further 4-6 to observe.
- A medium-size room with empty floor space. Ideally a room that normally might be expected to hold 20-30 people is a good rule of thumb. The odd chair or small table may be required for some elements.

Method:
1. Allow the Problem Owner to decide who is playing what role. For instance there may be one person designated as the Sales Team; another is the Client; a third is the Accounts Department and so on. Restrict the numbers of people they use so that in some circumstances one individual might represent a whole organisation or multinational company.

2. The Problem Owner lays out a sculpture using the people. He tells each component what they are doing and which direction they are facing. He can also simulate distance (both real and perceived) by placing people away from the centre. For example a Customer may not be looking at the Sales Team but is preoccupied with his/her own issues. Sometimes an individual in the sculpture might be standing high, raising a fist or even cowering in a corner. It's important to let this play develop until the Owner is happy that it represents their understanding of the current situation.

3. One of the components of the sculpture will be the Problem Owner themselves. At this stage a substitute (locum) stands in for them and is placed by the Owner accordingly. Once the Owner is happy with the components and the layout he stands back from the overall sculpture.

4. The Observers can now walk through the people and inspect. They can also ask different components what they feel about the positions they have been placed in.

This is where you get to hear what another organisation or team's perceptions might be of the situation.

5. Everyone is asked to remember their starting position. It can also help to photograph this from several angles as you are going to return to this later.

6. The Observers remodel the sculpture to what appears a better scenario. They can ask components which way they would feel more comfortable facing - depending on the things each is supposed to be considering. The Observers may also place one or two additional items (or remove some) in the process. During this process the Problem Owner is placed in the sculpture whilst the locum stands aside. This allows the Owner to feel the change that is happening.

7. The next step is to get everyone to remember this final position - it is the target state at the end of the change. Once again a photograph or two will help to record it. Now discussion can occur as to how each component gets to move from their starting position to this end state. A slow ballet will emerge as people are replaced in the starting gate and are then asked to move to the end. This may highlight potential collisions or breaks in communication. Overall it is an interactive piece. You can video the movement as an aide-memoire.

8. Players can use various objects that are in the room to connect components or to signify elements of the interaction. *I've known a power extension lead (unplugged) to be used as a rope wrapped round someone so that when it was pulled they start to twirl as they moved away.* There is huge opportunity for imagination here.

9. After a couple of rehearsals of the ballet the group will eventually settle on what is likely to work and why. The Problem Owner is then asked how they feel at the end state. To aid their understanding they also step back out of the sculpture and it is re-run with the locum so the owner can observe from the sidelines the overall effect.

10. Finally document the findings and recommendations sufficient for the Problem Owner to be able to take them away and work out a plan of action.

Case Study (4):

A young manager working in the supply chain for a major retailer was having difficulty envisaging how to implement change in his department. It appeared that one of the issues was his self-perception of what was required.

He therefore modelled the situation with a group of six players from outside his company. Some remodelling then occurred in due course. One of the benefits was that the group knew the individual but did not share the self-perception. In remodelling they were able to show him doing things he didn't think were possible but which the component parts of the sculpture were able to assure him were both OK and feasible.

After the remodelling was complete and an outline plan had been discussed about the way forward, the young man went out onto the balcony of the meeting room and lit an imaginary small bonfire into which he threw his preconceptions. In so doing he cleared the way in his own mind to be able to act differently and with confidence to deliver the solution he and the group had worked out.

Physically enacting change in these ways can be extremely powerful. In the case above the group were very supportive of the virtual bonfire and gave the young manager the space to carry it out without derision or questioning. This obvious support reinforced the change in mental attitude that was a key component of the solution to the initial problem.

Case Study (5):

A senior manager had been asked to project manage the build of Terminal 4 at Heathrow. Unfortunately this was going to be a very high pressure role and he had young family whom he wanted to spend time with as they grew up.

On the other hand the career implications were very significant and there was a great deal of prestige at stake.

The tensions between the employer (a very large civil engineering and construction company), the family and the client (BAA[22]) had to be dealt with somehow. Working on-site at the airport was inevitably going to play a huge role in the next couple of years of his life. Daily commuting from home simply wasn't an option and maintaining lines of communication was going to be critical.

The ensuing sculpture showed how the individual could redesign the engagement to satisfy all the relevant parties. It was possible to ask the person representing BAA how it felt and at the same time a couple of people representing spouse and children had a voice. The employer and its management were intrinsic to the solution.

The Problem Owner was able to leave the session (which had lasted about an hour) with a very clear idea of how to proceed and in what order to tackle things. They were now ready to accept the challenge of the project if they could achieve the solution suggested by the sculpture session.

Overall this demonstrates how this technique can blend the individual with the large organisation in a way that allows the different voices and perceptions to be surfaced. All this was achieved without a cast of thousands. The cost of doing the sculpture was a dozen man-hours and the new Heathrow Terminal was constructed without one particular family being torn apart.

Laddering

This is simply a way of building on ideas particularly in a group - although it is possible to use this as an individual. To coin a phrase you can chunk up - to a more generalised or

---

[22] BAA plc - the operator at Heathrow.

abstract view; or you can chunk down - to a concrete example.

Chunking up involves asking *"what is it an example of?"* whereas chunking down asks *"give some examples of ..."*

These are good ways to explore groups of conceptually related ideas. It's also a good way to move on from a crazy idea that you can't relate to and get to a more accessible option. Here's the dialogue that might follow in those circumstances: *"You have suggested X. You could think of that as an example of an S. What other kinds of S's are there? Y and Z? Would a Z help with this problem?*

Mind Maps

These are relatively simple to produce. You start with an idea (word or short phrase) in the centre and from it you add a short line to another word/phrase that springs to mind. The whole builds on what is there already and progressively fills up a large whiteboard.

You can also use mind-mapping software if you are doing the exercise on your own and want to capture the output electronically for use elsewhere. Some versions of software allow information to be captured at different levels so that the map can be collapsed or expanded.

My preferred method, in a group, is as follows:

1. The facilitator gives everyone a marker pen suitable for whiteboard use.

2. He/she writes the starting word in the centre of the board and everyone gathers around.

3. People individually dart in to add a word here or there, making sure that they put a connector from its predecessor. You can start a new cluster from the centre or add to an existing one or a branch from that.

4. They then step back and continue to view the building picture until something else springs to mind and they dart back in again.

5. When the board is full, everyone can step back and look for similarities (possibly at opposite sides) or clusters of suggestions that might be translated as metaphor for a solution to the objective.

6. Photograph the result.

The whole can be a bit like a feeding frenzy but that energy is helpful and allowing people to input their own contributions keeps everyone involved.

Rolestorming

This is merely a twist on *Brainstorming* (see page 95). Think of it as Brainstorming with Role-Play. (Personally I think that *Super Heroes* can work better if role play is going to be part of the mix - it all depends on how well people can put themselves into the shoes of the role model.) Here's how Rolestorming operates:

Each person in the group selects someone who is not present (but who they know pretty well) and assumes his or her role and general attitudes. (This could be someone else in the organisation, a typical customer, a well-known public figure or other person.)

Based on the attributes of this target person, the group member uses their attitudes, preferences and opinions to pretend they have a stake in the problem. As they put forward ideas they may say things such as *"My person would try to ..."* or *"My person would prefer ..."*

Super Heroes

This can be great fun and deliver good results but that depends on two things. First you have to prepare the ground and second the people playing have to have sufficient knowledge of their supposed character and be enthusiastic.

Requirements:

Facilitator to take notes and capture information.

A list of Super Hero characters - with some indication of what their special power(s) are.

Ideally you get the group who are going to be participating to pick their character the day before and come prepared to the workshop. Each person chooses a different character.

Method:

1. Once the problem has been described the floor is open to the Super Heroes.

2. Any character can step forward and explain how, using their superpower, they will overcome the problem.

3. Combinations of Super Hero may be called together to see if that gives further insight.

4. The outcomes are listed and the group can then revert to normal and discuss how these may be adapted to the objective.

In my experience this really can be excellent or a pretty dismal failure - there doesn't seem to be a middle ground. Let me tell you about one instance where it looked doomed to failure - only to be truly rescued by a Super Hero.

> A group of 16 MBA Students were taking part in a residential course and I was facilitating them through the technique. The night before the session they had selected their respective heroes. After breakfast the following morning we set about trying to tackle a difficult problem - but things were not going well. There was a complete lack of energy and virtually no ideas were forthcoming.
>
> However one of the group was missing and he had chosen the character of **Captain Chaos**. After 20 minutes of getting nowhere we were about to give up and move to something else when the door burst open

and **Captain Chaos** exploded into the room, falling over, knocking furniture flying and crying out - *"Don't panic - Captain Chaos is here ...!"*

The result was instantaneous. Everyone burst into peals of laughter, the energy levels shot up and suddenly the whole group was on fire to tackle the problem. As a result they produced a truly memorable intervention for the entire course of 150 people, which was talked about for years afterwards.

You should choose carefully when you use Super Heroes and make sure you have some really sparky people in the group before you get going.

Wynectics

This is a synthesis of techniques. Since its development in the mid-20th century *Synectics*[23] has been described as a method of identifying and solving problems that depends on creative thinking, the use of analogy, and informal conversation among a small group of individuals with diverse experience and expertise.

There are slightly differing views as to what constitutes a straightforward Synectics intervention. The most complex has:

1. Problem as Given (PAG)
2. Short analysis of the PAG
3. Purge
4. Problem as Understood
5. Excursion
6. Fantasy Force Fit (FFF) or Force Fit (FF)
7. Practical Force Fit (PFF)
8. Viewpoint or New Problem as Understood.

---

[23] This is a trademark of the Synectics Corporation who invented the original method.

Here we are going to deal with my own synthesised version *Wynectics* which takes elements from above (in particular the Excursion through to Viewpoint) but does so in a way that is relatively easy to execute. I don't believe in complexity for complexity's sake and this has the potential to be quite a wild ride. It also avoids some of the specialist roles of the classical version that are rather more demanding.

To begin with I am assuming that there is a truly great problem definition that has been arrived at through various forms of due diligence using methods earlier in this book.

So here we go. This is brainstorming on steroids and is the cluster of techniques I use most. It never fails to deliver creative ideas - even at no notice (remember the bit in the first chapter about the actuary who stopped me in the lunch queue?) It is also something that ordinary people find engaging and they rapidly get involved. Maybe that has something to do with the quirkiness of the Random Stimulus but groups from Southampton to Stornoway have grabbed the proverbial bull by the horns and delivered some outstanding ideas.

Even if you are not personally doing the creative exercises - getting your teams to understand how to go through Wynectics will be gold dust. You can do the whole thing as a group exercise in a few minutes or a couple of hours, with the pace being set by the facilitator. You can also do it on your own if that's all who is available.

Components:
- A Random Stimulus (read on for an explanation)
- Word Association
- Brainstorm
- Mind Map

Requirements:
- Whiteboard (the bigger the better)
- Flip-charts - I prefer to use two
- Post-It Notes
- Marker Pens - enough for everyone

- Camera - useful to capture the data once it is all on the board

Method:

1. First establish who the Problem Owner is and get an agreed Problem Definition using as much rigour as you can muster. As ever this is key to getting a good answer from what comes next.

2. Introduce the Problem to the group who are going to tackle the exercise.

   Now you are ready for some Random Stimulus - and in my experience the more random the better!

The science:

Using a random stimulus allows the brain more freedom to think differently. The fact that it is in no way related to the problem under scrutiny is essential. Sub-conscious processing will ultimately suggest linkages that you never imagined possible and it is this radical departure that we want to capture.

---

3. Sources of a Random Stimulus are many and varied. One way is to introduce something unconnected such as an item found lying on the ground. You can ask people to bring one odd thing to the session without telling them what it is going to be used for. I remember one occasion where a team member produced a toy *Star Trek Communicator* and that was the basis of a great session redesigning major processes for a mortgage lender.

   On the other hand you can carry around a few small odd items and get a team member to select one. My personal kit contains some very small model animals such as a lobster, a dragon and a pig. However what comes next is a step that I introduced and makes the whole process much more radical.

> **More science:**
>
> No matter what simple item is used as a stimulus the human brain is going to have embedded associations as to its attributes. So the following step creates an **impossible object** that breaks free from the shackles.

4. Let's assume your team member has chosen the lobster. Now we enter a stage where we do some Word Association. This involves simply listing the words the group associates with **lobster** or anything else that is subsequently written on the flip-chart by the Facilitator. Keep going until you have 20-30, it won't take more than a couple of minutes.

   At this point there will be a load of words or phrases that are completely random. If you like you can choose a second object and repeat the step.

5. From the resulting list(s) you are now going to select two completely unrelated words of phrases. You could ask a team member for a number between 1 and 20 and count up or down the list from a random start point. That gets one element of a compound name or phrase. *(I actually use several dice for them to roll so the number generation is quite random. They are allowed to roll up to 4 dice together so that can generate numbers from 1-24.)* Then repeat this with another number and a different start point **OR** ask someone else to suggest which one of the words you would like to use for the next stage of the exercise.

6. Now stick the two together and you will get some weird hybrid. I can recall a **Glass Handkerchief**; and a **Square Camel** amongst the many over the years. As you can probably guess these weird objects or imaginary creatures possess properties that challenge our everyday thinking and that's precisely why we've introduced them.

7. Now comes the first of two Questions. This is the Fantasy Force Fit

    In What Way Can We ... (IWWCW)?

    "In what way can we use a <Strange Object>?" Do this as a Brainstorm with the IWWCW Question as the problem. At this point we are not interested in the real problem - instead we are going on an excursion into the realms of fantasy and wackiness. And - believe me - the wackier the better at this stage because that will actually deliver the most powerful ideas. As you have already worked out by now a very large portion of being creative is about being open to metaphor and the richer the metaphor we can generate, the better.

    The group will come out with all sorts of ideas about ways to use purple mooncakes or cheese elephants.

8. The next step is to cluster the ideas from this brainstorm and select one grouping (you can always come back and do another if the first doesn't ultimately deliver, although I've only ever had to do that twice). Have a short description of what this grouping is about. Maybe the cheese elephants resulted in a group of ideas that collectively involved *stamping on toast* or something similar. So that's what we are going to use as a springboard for our Second Question.

    There's an interesting side-effect of doing these first couple of steps. Generally at the beginning of the session there is some apprehension in the room as to whether they will be able to solve the problem that has been pitched. By the time they have worked out ways to use a cheese elephant or whatever, the team's energy will be raised and there will be quite a bit of laughter. That bodes well as they have now relaxed and their minds are free to work at full throttle.

9. Now the second of the Questions

How Can We ... (HCW)?

Now we are going to mind-map how we can use this idea of *stamping on toast* to solve our real problem. So for this we can write up or signpost *"How Can We use X to solve Y?"* (In terms of classical Synectics this is the Practical Force Fit element.)

10. The following step is to do a Mind Map. (You could do a second brainstorm but in my experience mind-mapping is more powerful at this stage.) You want the group to cover a large whiteboard with a map that has X at its centre. If you've never experienced working with a team to mind map *stamping on toast* or something equally radical you are in for a treat.

    As noted in the Mind Map technique on page 102 a revolve of people diving in, adding a point or two and then stepping back will result in a fast and furious set of ideas. No validation is required at this stage.

Even more science:

Because we asked the simple question *How Can We use X to solve Y?* the map is likely to include things that can be done or suggest an action to be taken. People's sub-conscious will have suggested linkages without having to scratch their heads to any great degree.

That's all we need to generate a powerful metaphor related to the solving of our problem.

---

11. Finally step back from the finished map and select one or two things that can be done and try and relate these back to your problem and resource limitations. You can use voting or clustering to suggest areas for focus or investigation. Taking a picture of the completed map is a good record for future reference. The richness of ideas on one large whiteboard is frequently amazing.

Sometimes you can see combinations of ideas on opposite sides of the map that suggest really good options for investigation.

How long will it take?

Time to go through the whole Wynectics process can be as little as 15 minutes. So it's not a huge overhead. Typically a session will take around an hour. 5 minutes for Introduction; 5 minutes for the Word Association and 20 minutes each for the Brainstorm and Map. Add in some slack time between sections and that's 60 minutes well spent.

Big Group Stuff

Here are a couple of techniques that are more applicable on the very largest problems. They are unlikely ever to become embedded in your everyday - simply because of their scale. However it is useful to know a little bit about them so that should the need arise you can consider how to get hold of them for your organisation.

Metaplanning

This is a full process approach rather than focusing on one element of the CPS Cycle. I've never used it and only once come across someone else who had. Part of the reason is the sheer scale of resource that gets involved. However, for completeness, it is useful to have an overview so you can see how this kind of thing might function. It was originally developed in the 1970s by Metaplan GmbH who are a German consultancy firm. It is frequently used in clinical practices, research, and business contexts. The technique is taught in Metaplan's *Leadership & Organization Academy*[24].

Metaplanning consists of a number of communication tools to be used by groups searching for ideas and problem solutions. Uses include developing opinions and common understanding. It uses moderators who have been trained in the Metaplan-Method.

---

[24] http://www.metaplan.com/en/academy/

The method can be used in large-scale meetings or 'information markets'. Uses have included researching the attitudes and policy-making ideas of large numbers of people within a big organisation. One possible arrangement is to organise a 'fairground' of booths around a very large hall or exhibition space. Each booth deals with one predetermined theme, critical question or aspect. The booths are staffed by 'information butlers' who have been trained and manage the process.

The whole thing usually takes several months of prior planning and preparations. To avoid disillusionment there also has to be significant follow-up on the ideas surfaced. Not a cheap method but it's out there if you really need it.

Open Space

This is a method of engaging potentially huge groups of people to design change. It comes from The Open Space Institute[25] - a body that operates on some very interesting principles. Apparently when the concept of Open Space first began, early practitioners, used to elaborating on a good idea, wanted to embellish it. Harrison Owen (the founder) would caution, *"less is more; what can we take away and remain true to the spirit of what we are doing?"* Thus, they strive to 'keep it simple' by constantly reminding themselves of the essence of whatever they do.

In my eyes, Open Space Technology seeks to engineer change without telling people. The idea being that you can encourage people into change, you should not tell them to change. It is participative and operates on four principles:

- Whoever comes is the right people;
- Whatever happens is the only thing that could have;
- When it starts is the right time; and

---

[25] The Open Space web site is at http://www.openspaceworld.org

- When it's over, it's over.
- There is also the law of two feet. The law of two feet says *to take responsibility for what you care about; if you are neither learning nor contributing where you are, use your two feet and go somewhere else*.

Requirements:

Open Space Technology works best when these conditions are present:

- A real business issue that people care about, that it is something worth talking about.
- Mind-numbing complexity, such that no single person or small group fully understands or can solve the issue
- High levels of much diversity, in terms of the skills and people required for a successful resolution (far-reaching, boundless)
- Much passion and real or potential conflict, which implies that people genuinely care about the issue
- Real sense of urgency, meaning the time for decisions and action was 'yesterday',

To give you an idea it was first used when there were plans to drive a major new highway across lands that were part of a Native American reservation. Literally thousands of people were going to be affected in one way or another. As you can imagine the issues were highly complex and potentially volatile. The outcome was a design for execution that was owned by everyone.

Method:

People are invited to an Open Space event at which the problem is described. At the beginning of an open space the participants sit in a circle or in concentric circles for large groups (sometimes 300 or more).

It has four broad stages:

1. Opening Circle (agenda co-creation process at the start, without the facilitator helping / synthesising / suggesting / reducing topics).

2. Facilitator's explanation of principles and law (calling them guidelines, invitations, whatever suits the gathering).

3. Multiple conversations ideally happening around the same big space, ideally several discussion sessions across time (without the facilitator helping those groups). It is an iterative process - usually over a few consecutive days. Presentations are made on ideas until a consensus starts to emerge.

4. Closing Circle (comment and reflection).

Comments:

It is important to note that this is a very non-prescriptive method. We cannot go into something with other people and have preconceived ideas and then expect it to happen according to our plan. However we can use the above principles in our aims to start the change required. We will work with the people that are around us (assuming they don't use their two feet to go somewhere else!) Also we will not be prescriptive about what is going to happen.

In the past it is here that a lot of change has gone wrong. People have been so certain about the expected outcomes that when something else happens they are lost. We won't be lost because we have no expectation - other than that something will change. What and how will become clearer as it happens.

Note: This doesn't contradict the use of the desired destination that came out of the work on Problem Analysis. OpenSpace will not ignore it. What it will do is perhaps take everyone to that destination in ways that were never imagined. Also the interpretation that you subsequently place on elements of the solution may well change.

The argument that *"now is not the right time to start"* is commonly heard. But we can see differently that whenever we start is the right time. Moreover the ending may not come when we expect but so what? If we are using some Project Management method, we will know when everything is finished even if the timetable doesn't map onto the original plans.

Evaluation

Creative Evaluation

This was designed to assist in the organisation and evaluation of a large number of ideas. So that is why you would most likely want to use it, especially if one of the idea generation techniques has thrown up masses of options.

Requirements:

List of ideas; Group of assessors.

Method:

1. List the ideas from the idea generation process.

2. Using Roman Numerals, categorise each idea in one of three ways: **I** (simple), **II** (hard), and **III** (difficult).

3. The ideas in their categories are presented to management for additional evaluation.

Note: **Simple ideas** are those that can be implemented with minimum expenditure of time and money. **Hard ideas** will require slightly greater expenditure. Finally **Difficult ideas** require the greatest expenditure. It is up to the group to define the boundary between Hard and Difficult - probably with some input from the sponsor or senior management

Monte Carlo Estimating

This isn't creative in the way that idea generation can be. But it does give insight into the costs and benefits of some things you may be considering. One thing's sure - your Management Accountants will love it. It has its foundations in Monte Carlo Analysis whereby possible values in every step of a project cycle have randomised values based on an upper and lower limit. MCA usually runs for thousands of iterations to deliver a best-expected outcome value (usually the project duration). MCE gets there with less technology and some common sense.

The essence of this is to get a high confidence level about the costs and benefits of doing something new. More to the point it allows you to put values on things that aren't immediately valued. If you can make the hidden value visible you are more likely to realise it.

Requirements:

A good breakdown of the components of your solution (actions, investment/purchases etc.)

A similar breakdown of all the benefits it will deliver

A group to study the components and agree the estimates

Method:

The best way to achieve the requirements is to plan backwards from the ultimate objective. For each step, work out what will be required as an immediate predecessor. This will give you an inventory of components and how they link together.

For example you may have a final objective to complete a training programme. That requires you to have held a number of workshops. From this you can define how many and, looking at those, break down the components for each. And so on. For every component there can be a value - number of occurrences or the cost.

When looking at the outcomes you do the same by estimating the numbers involved and the value of each. This is achieved in this example by suggesting what change will have occurred for each attendee and how much impact that might have. Suppose from the training workshops maybe 50 attendees will gain X% improvement in sales. Each sale might have a value £Y and so on.

The key with the benefits is to look beyond the immediate cost savings or additional revenue. How about asking what the results might do to staff morale - and hence recruitment or retention costs? What might the changes do to customer satisfaction? By what percentage do you think it might move that up or down? Can you put some estimate on a 1% improvement in Customer Satisfaction in terms of value to the P&L ?

In essence this is very similar to project costing but the effort should look wider than direct costs and benefits.

Once you have the components laid out (or as complete a list as you can muster) then you can start applying some estimates to each one. Have a quick discussion with your group to get a consensus on each. Common sense really does work with this stuff and is surprisingly accurate when you do it one component at a time.

You are going to produce two sets of figures - a Worst Case and a Best Case. It's really an application of common sense. *"Will we get more than 50 or less than 50 at the worst case? Ditto for the best case?"* *"Will this cost us more than £1,000? More than £5,000?"* When you have a bracket, look at the mid-point to see if that gives a more accurate upper or lower figure. Keep going until you have two figures for everything.

Worst Cases for benefits are the lowest that you imagine might occur. And unit costs are the highest estimates you made.

Best Cases for benefits are the highest that you imagine might occur. Similarly the unit costs are the lowest that you estimated.

So we get two sets of calculations. Compile the components by simply adding or multiplying each one as appropriate. You can be very confident indeed that the actual costs and benefits sit somewhere on the range you have now described.

More to the point there is a high degree of confidence that the actual outcome will be somewhere around the mid-point. So if your worst case delivers benefit of £500k and the best case delivers benefit of £14 million - the mid-point is £7.25 million.

The critical point is to ensure that ALL the components that you identified are now on your execution plan - including delivery of the intangibles. You should be able to track these by relating them to the actions and steps from which they were expected to derive. So in our example you would not only be checking for the Training Workshops but also looking at the Customer Satisfaction surveys afterwards.

Much of this should tie in directly to project accounting - hence why the Management Accountants will love this. You are providing them with expected measures at every stage and that makes it easier to identify whether the overall project is on track to deliver the numbers. Early warnings about variance mean you can actually do something about it.

Also by deriving values for the intangibles you make them real. Questions can be asked of the implementation team to ensure they are not overlooked. Overall this leads to better understanding of what is being developed. It can also change the priorities between projects - see the second case study below,

Based on many years experience it is highly unusual for projects to engage in this depth of analysis but when they do they nearly always over-deliver against the original expectations. Moreover they also tend to stop the project scope creep that is endemic to many change programmes. The reason? Surfacing measurable expectations at every stage makes it a lot easier to identify when things are going off track.

Case Study (6):

Professor Antonella Sorace is an internationally renowned developmental linguist who works at the University of Edinburgh. She is passionate about development of language. Moreover she knows that kids who are brought up to be bi-lingual (possibly because they have parents from different cultures) have better cognitive skills. Better cognition is also valuable in later life - the person that has it is more equipped to deal with complexity and cultural differences. So Antonella decided to launch an initiative to provide support for the parents of these children and called it *Bilingualism Matters*.

That was the easy bit. But how to persuade people to fund such an esoteric piece of work?

In the space of an afternoon we developed a business case using Monte Carlo estimates of the numbers of people affected across Scotland to begin with; the impact of better cognition on their learning; and capacity in work. Finally we looked at the value this represented in additional capacity for the workforce and the impact that might have on productivity. Using some simple ideas we can value productivity relative to earnings - after all most employers expect a multiple return on staff cost.

What the result showed was a benefit to the Scottish economy alone that was worth £millions - and all from running a relatively inexpensive support network to enhance the language skills of a number of kids.

Case Study (7):

In 2002 the retail arm of the Royal Bank of Scotland had an annual budget of well over £100 million for running programmes of change - and a list as long as your arm of projects competing to be done. How do you decide priorities in a case like this?

I got them started by looking at how to measure all the proposals using the sorts of steps outlined in the Method above. Numbers of people involved, impacts on costs and savings, how much it might move customer satisfaction and so on.

Surprisingly this method had never been used previously. The batting order had always been drawn up by Finance based solely on legislative or regulatory imperative and after that purely by looking at the effect on the Share Price. We pointed out that this did **not** conform to the stated objectives of looking after three groups of stakeholders, the Customers, the Staff and the Shareholders. According to the bank's mission statement all were supposed to have equal status.

Feeding all the data into a model allowed disparate projects to be compared. Setting aside the mandatory ones, there was still a significant budget and it was a case of optimising that to deliver the best overall benefit.

Some projects would need to use the same resources and note was taken of what those were so that scheduling conflicts could be avoided. There were only limited numbers of certain specialists available internally or constraints on access to IT or other resources. Also some of these could not be hired in from elsewhere. This was all pretty straightforward stuff.

Finally the projects were sorted according to expected deliverable benefits - which included the value of the intangibles such as staff morale and customer retention. To the surprise of the senior management a number of pet projects got kicked way down the batting order as a result. Also the value of the overall portfolio was checked against the initial project benefits that had been suggested by the various owners.

Because they were now considering intangibles it became possible to estimate the **additional value** that might be realised over a period of years. Even the mandatory projects went through this to see what else they could deliver. Overall the additional benefit had an NPV of more than £500 million. That's a significant return for a creativity exercise costing less than £100k.

As an aside the emphasis on paying attention to Customers and Staff, if it had been spread across the whole organisation and followed through with rigour, might have prevented the bank hitting the financial buffers in such a spectacular fashion in 2009. So paying attention and being creative has the potential to avert some astronomical risks.

Sticking Dots

You can buy packs of sticky dots in most stationery stores. They come in different sizes and a variety of colours. This technique assumes you have such a supply to hand, although if you are using a whiteboard or flip-chart, coloured marker pens can work equally well.

Method:

1. A list of ideas is displayed on flip-chart or wall.

2. Each group member is given a limited number of votes in the form of adhesive dots. (The usual ratio is 10% of the number of ideas listed. Thus 6 votes across 60 ideas.)

3. Allocation can be multiple to one idea or equally spread across several. The dots are stuck alongside the idea listed. This gives a very quick visual representation of the weight of votes in favour.

4. Votes are tallied and the winning idea(s) is/are selected for further analysis or implementation.

An alternate way of doing this would be to use an online voting system although with large numbers of ideas the overhead of preparing the survey could be quite heavy. Nevertheless this alternative would allow people from around the globe to contribute votes if that was appropriate. Even a complete list with an email response would work if someone centrally coordinates the replies.

The benefit of the method is that it is cheap and cheerful, The downside is that there is little other than subjective evaluation going on so it is often useful to have a discussion around this point before the voting commences, That way the group members are more likely to think about resource usage, practicality and other constraints.

Weighting Systems

This is a straightforward way of assigning different weights to different components of a proposed solution. The best way is to use some form of tabulation - a spreadsheet works well - with two more columns than there are alternatives.

List the Criteria in the first column and have a discussion about what weight should be applied to each criterion. Then enter that value in the second column.

The rest is a function of the first two - where for each alternative the value for **what is**, is given and, to deliver a weighted value, that is multiplied by the factor in the second column.

Here's a visual depiction:

Criteria	What Should Be (relative importance)	Alternative #1		Alternative #2		etc
		What is	SubTotal	What is	SubTotal	
Cost per unit ...	5					
Time to implement ...	3					
	6					
	etc					

Figure 7 Weighting

You can develop more sophisticated models depending on the nuances of the situation. Sometimes these can be quite informative and it is useful to review the results after a first pass. I often find that reveals the weightings are slightly out of kilter but they can easily be tweaked. Don't forget that tweaking **isn't** a mechanism to deliver a favourite as winner but sometimes our original estimate of relative values for different criteria is called into question. So revisiting that is not a bad thing.

Farewell to the Harlequin Bat

Put more simply - the conclusion.

We started this journey by introducing some strange concepts - maybe that was why you picked up the book in the first place. Now you should have a solid understanding of how this stuff knits together. What to expect and what not.

Moving forward it is really a case of going out 'on the road' and getting in some practice. Like all learner drivers you may be a little nervous but there is truly nothing to worry about. Don't be afraid to turn back to sections and re-read techniques before applying them, nobody is going to criticise you for being careful. However, if my experience and that of thousands of other people I've mentored in Creativity over the last 20 years is anything to go by, you will rapidly pick it up and start to evolve your own style. After all, the only thing that you need to keep in mind is WHY you are doing this at all. Presumably that is because you or your organisation wants some tricky problem(s) to be solved. When you start to see how the process gets to grips with even the seemingly impossible, then you will feel hugely rewarded.

I really do mean that last bit about rewards. There is always something worthwhile about cracking a problem that has been frustrating things. Besides if you are overseeing a team that are doing it, there's a lot of kudos coming your way.

Also - don't be afraid if things don't always go to plan - just remember where you are in the CPS Cycle and you won't go far wrong. Most stages can be iterated until you are sure you are on the right track. After all it is only once you get to the Execution Stage(s) that it is likely you are going to be using up large amounts of resource. A £10 million programme of work may have started from a series of workshops to decide what to do and why. So keep in mind that spending a little more time on getting that bit right is going to save way more money than rushing to start on some artificial deadline.

And finally - remember that a Square Camel never gets the hump but it may be that Addictive Pigs have frequent flyer programmes. So go flying with your own creations and those that your team construct. Flights of fancy are not just fun - they really can save your bacon.

Above all please remember that you don't have to try and be anyone else. I'm not asking you to change - just to understand and use that understanding to allow creativity to happen. In so doing you will move from learner driver to a more than competent person in the heavy traffic.

Index

A

Abrasive, 12
Addictive Pig, 1, 79
Affluent, 42
Agenda
   Co-creation, 120
Alter-Ego, 46
American Express, 43
Analogies, 44
Analogy, 2, 87
Analysis, Monte Carlo, 122
Analytical, 38, 39
Army, Australian
   Modernisation Branch, 46
Arrogant, 12
Association, Free, 85
Assumption Reversals, 81
Assumption(s), 8, 12, 41, 42, 64, 65, 70
Attribute, 40, 44, 71, 109, 114
   Personal, 25
Attribute Listing, 81

B

BAA plc, 107
Bandler
   Dr. Richard, 88
Beach, 93
Behaviour, 35, 41, 47, 48, 66
   Human, 11
Behavioural, 42
Belbin
   Team Roles, 44
Bias
   Cognitive, 37, 63
   Confirmation, 49
Big Group Stuff, 117
Bilingualism Matters, 125
Binoculars, Flipping the, 55
Bíró
   László, 6
Blockchain, 39
Bonfire
   Imaginary, 106
Boundary Examination, 64, 65
Bracket, 123
Brain, 41
Brainstorm, 112
Brainstorming, 95
   Private, 89
Brainstorming, Reverse, 98
Brainwriting, 98, 101
   Game, 99
Bridge the Gap, 12
British Computer Society, 4

C

Captain Chaos, 111, *See also* Super Heroes
Case Study
   (1), 46
   (2), 46
   (3), 17
   (4), 106
   (5), 106
   (6), 125
   (7), 125
Causes, Possible, 69
CEO
   Powerful, 3
Channel
   Auditory, 92
   Kinæsthetic, 92
   Visual, 92
Checklists, 51, 83
Cheese Elephants, 115
Chunking
   Down, 108
   Up, 108
Circle
   Closing, 120
   Opening, 120
Coach(ing), 29
Cognition, 125
Cognitive
   Skills, 125
   Style, 30
Cognitive Bias. *See* Bias, Cognitive

Colour Blindness, 78
Comfort Zone, 43, 64, 79
Communications, 4, 12
  Difficulties, 35, 45
  Powerful, 74
  Tools, 117
Concepts, Radical, 1
Conclusion, 130
Confirmation Bias. *See*
  Bias:Confirmation
Conflict, 36, 88, 119, 126
Connection
  Psychological, 72
Conscious, 52, 67, 90
Consciousness, 94
  Stream of, 85
Consensus, 50, 120, 123
Constraints, Embracing, 65
Construction
  Company, 107
Constructs, Metaphorical, 88
Conversations, 55, 71, 111, 120
Cookery, 2
Co-ordination
  Poor, 4
Core Competence, 80
Courage, 2
CPS Cycle, 16, 69, 117, 130
  Illustration, 17
CPS Solution
  the right, 18
Crawford, C.C., 101
Crazy Idea, 58, 100, 108
Creation Theory, 41
Creative
  Style, 12, 29
  Swiping, 9, 56
Creativity
  Definition of, 8
  Embedding, 2, 3, 15, 16, 40
  Hierarchy, 2
  Negative, 98
  Practitioner, 1
Customer
  Comparative, 51
  Service, 42
Customer(s), 42

D

da Vinci
  Leonardo, 38
Darwinian Evolution, 41
Daydreaming, 52
D-Day, 4
de Bono
  Edward, 80
Decision-making, 70
Dellinger
  Dr Susan, 33
Desert Storm, Operation, 4
Dillon
  Karen, 10
Dimensions, 57
  Three-dimensional, 60
  Two-dimensional, 58
Direct To Garment (DTG), 66
Disseminator, 44
Diverse, Diversity, 32, 40, 47, 55, 111
Doodle, 73, 75, 76
Downturn, Economic, 41
Drawing, 75
Drive, Learning how to, 11
Driving Lessons, 11, 69
Duplicates, 97
Dyson
  James, 6

E

Edinburgh
  University of, 125
Edwards
  Betty, 74
Ego, 1
Emotional Intelligence, 103
Emotional State, 89
Enemy
  of Creativity, 32
Engineering, Royal Academy of, 4
Environmentally, 67
Envisaging, 80
Estimating, Monte Carlo, 121
Ethical, 67
Evaluation, 121
Evaluation
  Creative, 121
Executive(s), 2, 10, 11, 31, 45, 52, 54, 63, 70, 95
Executive(s), Senior, 2, 42, 72

Executive, Chief, 46
Exit State, 92
Experience, Jump-starting, 56
Expert, 2, 16, 21, 68
Explorer, 44

F

Facilitator, 23, 89, 96, 98, 99, 100, 103, 104, 108, 110, 112, 114, 120
Failure
   to build creatively, 6
Family, 36, 107
FAQs, 51
Feedback
   Visual, 76
Figure of Speech, 87
Financial Services, 42
Finger Paints, 77
Fishbone
   Diagram, 67
Five W's and H, 52
Flip-chart, 77, 95, 112, 114, 127
Food, 14
Football Teams, 29
Forager, 44
Force Fit, 111
   Fantasy, 111, 115
   Practical, 111, 116
Formula 1, 9

G

Games, Invictus 2018, 46
Glass Handkerchief, 1, 114
Goal Reversal, 86
Google, 21, 43
Gravity, 14
Grinder
   John, 88
Groove Tendency, 41
Group Technique, 22
Groupthink, 32, 80

H

Harlequin Bat, 1, 57, 79, 130
Harvard Business Review, 10
Hats
   Metaphorical, 45
Head Bending, 89

Heathrow Airport
   Terminal 4, 106
Human Sculpture, 102
   End state, 105
   Locum, 104, 105
   Video aide-memoire, 105
Hynoptic Technique, 88
Hypnosis, Self-, 91
Hypnotist, 88

I

Idea Generation, 21, 79
   Selecting Techniques, 27
Ideas
   Difficult, 121
   Hard, 121
   Simple, 121
Ideating, 18
Ideation, 102
Individual Technique, 22
Infallible, 2
Information Butlers, 118
Innovation
   Hierarchy, 2
Interpreter, 73, 75
   Right Brain, 75
Intuitive, 39
Ishikawa
   Diagram, 67
   Kaora, 67
Isle of Wight, 66
IT Development
   Agile, 30
   Waterfall, 30

J

Jensen
   J.V., 88

K

Kepner
   Chuck, 68
Kepner-Tregoe, 68
Kidd
   Patrick, 46
Kinæsthetic, 71, 92
Kirton
   Adaption-Innovation
   Inventory, 45

Dr. Michael, 12, 45
Knowledge
 Applying, 3
 Hierarchy, 2
 Imperfect, 3
Kudos, 130

L

Laddering, 107
Language, 74
 problem, 76
Lateral Thinking. See
 Thinking:Lateral
Law of two feet, 119
Layer(s), 77
Leader, Creative, 32
Leadership
 Weak, 4
Lego, 43
Lens
 Seeing the world through, 71
Lewis Carroll, 57
Listening, Art of, 50
Literal, 87

M

Machinery
 Crazy, 1
Magazine Rack, 56
Management
 Senior, 121
Management Accountant, 121
Marker Pens, 95, 96, 108, 112, 127
Marketing, 13
Mass-Market, 42
MBDA, 46
McKenna
 Paul, 88
Metaphor, 62, 71, 77, 87, 115, 116
 Visual, 75
Metaplan
 GmbH, 117
 Method, 117
Metaplanning, 117
Micawber, Mr, 54
Mind Map, 112
Mirroring, 57, 88

Mobile Device, 82
Monte Carlo Analysis. See
 Analysis, Monte Carlo
Monte Carlo Estimating. See
 Estimating, Monte Carlo
Mooncakes, 115
Morphological Analysis, 57
Mortgage
 Sub-prime, collapse, 4

N

Neuro-Linguistic Programming (NLP)
 Techniques, 88
Neuroscience, 40
Nominal Group Technique, 22, 90
Normal Distribution, 12
Notebook, Reporter's, 52
NPV, Net Present Value, 127

O

Objectives, Exaggerated, 84
Open Space
 Technology, 118
Operational, 39
Organisation
 Your, 1
Overlord, Operation, 4
Owen
 Harrison, 118

P

Panacea, 89
Paradox, Logical, 81
Pathways
 Neural, 88
Perception, 88
Photocopy, 76
Pig, Addictive. See Addictive Pig
Pizza, 93
Planning & Preparation, 4
Playful, 11, 47
Playfulness, 45
Possible Causes. See Causes, Possible
Posters, 14
Post-It Notes, 61, 95, 96, 101, 112

Practicality, 128
Preconceptions, 41, 106
Presentations, 14
Problem Analysis, 18, 21
   Cycle, 68
Problem Definition
   Selecting Techniques, 26
Problem Distinctions, 69
Problem Owner, 53, 62, 96, 97, 103, 104, 106, 107, 113
Problem Statement, 96
Product Improvement Checklist, (PICL), 79
Psycho-Geometric Theory, 33
Psychology
   Personal, 29

R

R&D, 13
Random Stimulus, 101, 112
Rapanui, 43, 66
Recipe Book, 2
Redefinitional, 64
Reflection, 55, 62, 120
Reframing, 62
Regulatory, 126
Regulatory, Change, 66
Relational, 38, 39
Relevant Changes, 69
Remodelling, 106
Representation
   Internal, 88
Reticence, 87
Reversals, 90
Reverse Brainstorming. *See* Brainstorming, Reverse
Right Brain, 74, 75
   Communication, 74
   Connecting with, 74
   Drawing, 73, 74
Right People, 119
Right Time, 119
Royal Bank of Scotland, 125
Ryanair, 43

S

Sand
   Head in the, 55
SCAMPER, 84

Science, 52, 74, 100, 113, 114, 116
   Rocket, 11
Scottish
   Economy, 125
Segmentation, 42
Shapes
   Box, 34
   Circle, 36
   Rectangle, 35
   Squiggle, 36
   Triangle, 35
Share Price, 126
Shareholders, 126
Sharing, 62
Skidpan, 69
Software
   Mind-Mapping, 108
Sorace
   Professor Antonella, 125
Southampton, 112
Space, 14
Sponsor, 121
Square Camel, 1, 12, 79, 114
Sticking Dots, 127
Stimulus, Random. *See* Random Stimulus
Stop! Technique, 23
   Alternative uses, 24
Stornoway, 112
Story Boards, 14
Strength-test, 2
Stuckness
   Mental, 8
Style, 9, 14, 25, 28, 29, 31, 32, 36, 39, 44, 70, 130
Sub-conscious, 29, 52, 76, 91, 113, 116
Super Heroes, 46, 109
Super-mind, 80
Supplier, 91, 103
SurveyMonkey, 22
Synectics, 23, 111
   Corporation, 111
Synthesiser, 44

T

Tear-Down, Method, 98
Techniques
   Selecting, 26, 27

Technology, 63, 66, 122
Think Tech, 63
Thinking
  Lateral, 80
  Vertical, 80
Through the Looking Glass, 57
Tower, Grenfell (2017), 5
Tradesman, 91
Traits
  Negative, 34, 35, 36
  Positive, 34, 35, 36
Tregoe
  Benjamin, 68
Tumble Dryer, 8

U

Unconscious, 8, 91, 94
Unfamiliarity, 64
Universe
  Crazy, 57

V

Validation, Confirmation Bias
  Part 1, 49
  Part 2, 69
Validation, Technique, 22
Van Gundy
  Arthur B. Jr., 79
Verbal, 74
Vision, Normal, 78
Votes, 127

W

Weaknesses
  Examination of, 98
Whiteboard, 95, 108, 112, 116, 127
Why?, Repeated, 54
Wikipedia, 21
Word Association, 112, 114
Wynectics, 21, 23, 64, 86, 111

Y

YouTube, 21

Z

Zero Gravity, 14

About the author:

Rob Wherrett is Executive Chairman of Zymolysis - a niche management consultancy - and he heads its Executive Coaching practice.

More than anything he recognises that in order for change to be successful it has to address the right problems. In so doing he helps clients to save massively on their resources, while at the same time making life better for everyone involved.

He is recognised as being unique in the breadth of his experience which stretches from psychometrics and personal inventories, through creativity, into the complete range of execution planning and delivery, with world-class programme governance at its heart. Rob is passionate about doing the right thing first time and making sure the quality of solution is excellent. This resulted in a number of accolades when he was heading product development for a UK Financial Services organisation. Subsequently he has also helped many very large organisations get to grips with complex problems and deliver world-class solutions.

Today he divides his time between developing Executive Leaders; teaching and consulting on Creativity; and running Not-for-Profit organisations. He is a Fellow of both the UK Institute of Leadership & Management and the Royal Society of Arts as well as being an assessor for the Institute of Consulting[26].

His wide-ranging sector experience covers:

Leisure; Higher Education; Non-Food Retail; Financial Services; Military/Defence; Central Government; Immigration; International Development; Healthcare; Hospitality and Non-Profit

---

[26] Part of the UK's Chartered Management Institute

By the same author:

The Compleat Biz: The Business Model for the 21st Century (2009)

In Search of the Two-Headed Elephant: Tales from Malawi (2014)

More creativity material is available from
http://executive-2020-coaching.com/

www.ingramcontent.com/pod-product-compliance
Lightning Source LLC
Chambersburg PA
CBHW052025290426
44112CB00014B/2378